WildLife

Other Books By Pat Neal

Wildlife Volume 1

The Fisherman's Prayer

Wildlife Volume 2 The Mountain Pond

Wildlife Volume 3 Fisherman's Holidays

WildLife

*Volume 4: The Wilderness
Gossip Columnist*

PAT NEAL

WILDLIFE
VOLUME 4: THE WILDERNESS GOSSIP COLUMNIST

iUniverse books may be ordered through booksellers or by contacting:

iUniverse
1663 Liberty Drive
Bloomington, IN 47403
www.iuniverse.com
844-349-9409

ISBN: 978-1-6632-6776-4 (sc)
ISBN: 978-1-6632-6777-1 (e)

Print information available on the last page.

iUniverse rev. date: 12/19/2024

For Gary and Charlotte.

INTRODUCTION

The Olympic Peninsula has been called the last frontier. In 1978 I was hired by the Washington State Office of Archaeology and Historic Preservation to conduct a cultural resource survey of the Olympic Peninsula, identifying and locating historic sites, structures, and artifacts and nominating eligible properties to the National Register of Historic Places.

The 1970s were an exciting time for historic research on the Olympic Peninsula. The Ozette village, called "the American Pompeii" because it had been buried in mud, was being excavated. The Makah Museum at Neah Bay was built to house the artifacts salvaged from the dig. The Manis Mastodon site near Sequim had produced a spearpoint in an extinct elephant rib that made it the oldest evidence of human occupation in the Pacific Northwest at the time. While these discoveries were being made, my research located and identified a three-hole outhouse, which proved to be the largest known pioneer restroom facility in the Olympic Mountains.

However, the real treasure I discovered during this research was the sons and daughters of the Native Americans who were hanging on to their traditional ways and the children of European pioneers who came into this country in the late 1800s. By the 1970s these children were senior citizens who remembered the past in vivid detail. They were what every historian treasures: primary sources. My job was to remember everything they said.

In 1998, I began writing a weekly wilderness gossip column that traces the history of the Olympic Peninsula, a land that was thought to have inexhaustible fisheries and timber, to the present, where our natural resources are threatened, endangered, or extinct. These stories are about the end of the last frontier.

This book is a year's worth of wilderness gossip columns written from my experience as a historian and life as a guide on the rainforest rivers of the Olympic Peninsula. I hope you like them.

I would like to thank Brian McLean and Kelley Lane, editors at the *Peninsula Daily News* for their kind assistance in presenting these stories.

Pat Neal
Hoh River, Washington

November 2024

TABLE OF CONTENTS

A NEW ADVENTURE SPORT

There's a new outdoor adventure sport making waves all across this emerald-green paradise we call the Olympic Peninsula. This recreational activity combines the risk of Russian roulette with the drama of a demolition derby. We call it tsunami watching. While this new sport was pretty harmless last weekend, the potential for pain is always there.

To participate in this new adventure sport, all you need to do is keep tuned to your news or weather source. When they tell you to stay off the beach and head for high ground because a tsunami may hit, load up the family, pets, and a picnic and head for the beach to watch the tsunami come in.

I know what you're thinking. Tsunami watching is crazy, but if the crowds of people at the beach ignoring the tsunami warning last Saturday are any indication, this new sport of tsunami watching is taking the country by storm.

Throughout history and around the world, people have told stories of floods. Here on the Olympic Peninsula, every Native American tribe has a shared tradition of devastating floods that have been confirmed by geological and archaeological research. One evening in the distant past, the Quileute noticed a wave that stretched across the horizon coming toward shore. The Quileute gathered their possessions in canoes and tied the canoes together. Some of the canoes broke loose when the wave hit. They floated east to the other side of the Olympic Mountains.

The Makah said the water rose until Cape Flattery became an island, then receded, leaving whales stranded on dry land. The water rose again. The Makah got in their canoes and floated away. Many drifted north to Vancouver Island. As the water receded, canoe-loads of people crashed into treetops. Many lives were lost.

Along the Strait of Juan de Fuca, the S'Klallam were warned a flood was coming. A man told them to build some strong canoes that would handle a storm. People said they would just walk up into the mountains if the flood came. It began to rain. The rivers turned to salt water as the sea level rose. Flooding creeks and rivers kept people from walking to higher ground. Some got away in their canoes with a supply of food and water. Only those who were able to tie themselves to the top of the Unicorn Peak up near Hurricane Ridge were saved. In fact, archaeologists determined that the S'Klallam village of Tse-whit-zen on the waterfront in present day Port Angeles was hit by up to five tsunamis in its 2,700-year history.

Those tsunamis were most likely caused by a Cascadia Subduction event, where the Juan de Fuca plate slips underneath the North American continent every five hundred years or so. This causes earthquakes and their associated tsunamis, the last of which occurred on January 26, 1700.

There was no tsunami warning siren, Coast Guard airlift, or National Guard at the time. We can only speculate at the massive loss of life that must have occurred.

These days, we live in an age of information, but we'd just as soon ignore the information. We are not about to let some foreign global tidal wave ruin a three-day weekend. So when the nanny state tells us to stay off the beach because of the tsunami, we head for the beach to watch it. It's a new adventure sport.

January 19, 2022

2

DE-EXTINCTING THE HUNDRED-POUND SALMON

Who says there's no good news? Recently, scientists claimed they are on the verge of bringing the woolly mammoth back from extinction. These large, hairy, elephant-like creatures were said to have gone extinct, along with mastodons, ground sloths, dire wolves, and a host of other prehistoric monsters, called Pleistocene megafauna, somewhere between 10,000 and 15,000 years ago.

Theories vary on perpetrators of this mass extinction, but the usual suspects (humans and climate change) have been repeat offenders. Evidence of humans hunting these massive Pleistocene creatures can be found in Washington's own Manis Mastodon Site located near Sequim. There, the remains of bison and caribou were discovered along with a spear point made from mastodon bone 13,800 years ago. It was found embedded in a mastodon rib, making the site one of the earliest barbecues in North America.

Whether humans were responsible for the extinction of Pleistocene megafauna is a debatable point of circumstantial evidence. Maybe it's only a coincidence these large creatures went extinct shortly after the migration of humans from Siberia and Asia across the Bering Land Bridge to North America. Then again, it could fit a pattern of human behavior that has been displayed throughout their history around the world. When a land bridge formed between Australia and Tasmania by lower sea levels in the last ice age, Aboriginal people wasted no time hunting the megafauna into extinction. Currently, humans are trying to make up for these extinctions with a process called de-extinction.

Colossal Biosciences, a Dallas-based company, is working on a plan to bring back the woolly mammoth by 2027. They hope to do this by genetically engineering cells from an Asian elephant into a creature with a furry coat and a fat layer that can survive in the Arctic. Their initial herd of one hundred woolly mammoths would be turned loose in the Arctic, where Colossal Biosciences imagines they would combat climate change. If this plan is successful, Colossal Biosciences hopes to de-extinct other creatures, such as the Tasmanian tiger and the dodo bird. All of this begs the question: what will it do for fishing?

The Elwha River in Washington state was once famous for its hundred-pound Chinook salmon. Historically, hundred-pound salmon occurred in rivers from the Columbia River to the Yukon. These giant Chinook were wiped out in the 1900s by a combination of habitat destruction, dams, irrigation, and overharvesting. Efforts to restore the hundred-pound salmon along with a host of other threatened or endangered species of fish in Washington have been a colossal, billion-dollar failure. A March 10, 2024 *Seattle Times* story reported that Washington state is spending a million dollars a day replacing culverts, many in streams that salmon cannot reach. It's not unlike the $351.4 million Elwha Dam removal project. This has been a colossal failure where Chinook are unable to reach their historic pristine spawning grounds in the upper Elwha due to rock slides and the unwillingness of the fisheries' comanagers to introduce fertilized eggs and juvenile and adult spawning Chinook into the upper watershed.

It would be nice to think that our hundred-pound salmon could be returned to our waters with Colossal Biosciences' de-extinction protocol, but there is a simpler solution. Recently, a world-record 105-pound Chinook was caught in Chile! It's ironic that the world-class Chinook salmon fishing in Chile was created by planting eggs from Washington state fish hatcheries in their rivers back in the

1980s. Maybe we could ask Chile if we could borrow some of their hundred-pound salmon eggs and recreate their incredible salmon fisheries here in Washington. We'll thank ourselves later if we do the right thing now.

January 22, 2024

3

I HATE MICE

I consider myself a humane person. I brake for crows. I swerve to miss squirrels who employ the practice of using automobiles to crush spruce cones they have dropped in the road, then scurry about the blacktop, stuffing their cheeks with the loose seeds. I have always supported a spay-neuter program for pet dumpers. These are humans who leave defenseless domestic animals out in the woods to be preyed upon by wild creatures or die of slow starvation. This concern for the welfare of all creatures great and small went out the window one morning upon discovering a warm winter fishing hat in a drawer, filled to the brim with goose down from a pillaged sleeping bag. My hard-weather gear had become a nursery for a family of mice.

While in modern times mice have been reviled for their role in the spread of pestilence, disease, and famine, throughout history and around the world, mice have played an important role in folk tales that have no relation to their size. In various mythological legends, mice have trapped the sun, stolen fire for humans, given humans leadership over the animals, found mates for lonely suitors, provided wisdom, and been accused of witchcraft.

One of the most poignant accounts of the mouse's role in human history was not a legend at all but a well-documented account from the Second World War of the last century. The 48th Panzer Corps under General Ferdinand Hein had run out of fuel during the Battle of Stalingrad. It was a major turning point in the war. The Germans had buried 102 tanks in pits to protect them from the Russian winter. When the Russians counterattacked, the Germans tried to start their tanks, but mice had chewed the ignition wires. Some of the tanks burst into flames when the Germans started them. Only forty-two tanks survived.

My own version of a mouse attack on the Eastern Front occurred one winter when I started my truck and turned on the heater to let it warm up. All too soon, the interior was filled with the distinctive aroma of a burning mouse nest and its inhabitants. We had to roll down the windows to breathe. It was freezing cold, but I couldn't use the heater because it was jammed up with a burning mouse nest.

People say I should get a cat to get rid of the mice. But I love cats, too much to have one. There are just too many predators, from great horned owls to coyotes, for a kitty to be safe around here. Efforts to eliminate mice are as varied as the human imagination. A friend once tried poison. I would not recommend this practice to anyone. When he offered a cup of coffee, I noticed the cap had been left off his fancy electric coffee grinder. Mixed into the coffee beans was a scattering of the bright blue mouse poison pellets.

I said I already had enough coffee, thanks. It seems as if the mice these days are just as crafty and persistent as they ever were. I have tried trapping the mice. This can be a painful lesson in self-defeat and futility. More is not better. I know that after setting two dozen mousetraps in the house and forgetting where they were. That midnight trip to the bathroom takes on a whole new drama when you snap your trap on your toe. I tripped about half the mousetraps, and the mice stayed out of the others. By now, I'm convinced the only sure way to deal with mice in your house is to move to another house.

January 31, 2017

A GOOD HORSE

Back on the farm, we used to say that all the animals go to heaven. There was a great reminder of this eternal truth when a picture came in the mail last week. I was holding a lead rope on a donkey with my two sisters on her back. The donkey was named Cinderella by someone with a weird sense of humor. The legend says the cross on the burro's back is a reminder of the time a donkey carried Christ into Jerusalem then followed him to Calvary, where the shadow of the cross fell on the poor burro and stayed there ever since. It's a beautiful story, but if Jesus had to ride Cinderella to Jerusalem, he might have been bucked off long before he made it there.

Cinderella was a bucking burro. We kids thought she must have packed the Antichrist. Bucking was not her only talent. She had a way of brushing off a rider by going into the brush and knocking them off with low-hanging tree limbs. Or she would gallop into her feeding shed that was just tall enough for her. She knew how to get rid of a human in a hurry, so you'd better jump off before you were knocked off.

Still, riding a burro was better than riding a cow. I know that now. This was especially true for the razor-backed Holstein steers we used to get cheap from the dairy farms. You know the ones. They'd be about fifteen hundred pounds or more, of which five hundred pounds was bones. You had to wait until they were asleep to get on one of these critters. You had to hang on once they woke up because they were not going to be happy. But if you could stay on a bucking burro, you had a chance on a bucking steer—until they figured out how to brush you off in the woods that is.

Then, one magic day, we got a horse. People were always giving us horses. Free horses are a lot like free trucks or boats or dogs. They have issues. Still, there's nothing better than having a good horse under you. It certainly beats having a horse roll over on top of you, especially if you are in a swamp or crossing a creek, but more on that later.

As kids, we were very proud of the fact that we could train our horses ourselves. We taught them to do pretty much whatever they wanted. They wanted to run fast. But if you could ride a burro or a steer, riding a horse was easy. The only problem was getting on top of them. That's when the trouble started. Just when you put a foot in the stirrup, the horse would wake up and start crow-hopping in circles while kicking and trying to bite you in the rear.

If you actually made it in the saddle, you had better hang on because there was only one speed and that was full throttle—until you came to a body of water. That's when the horse decided to stop, drop, and roll, which could bust up the saddle and the rider if you stayed on. Then again, if you jumped off, you would have to get back on so you'd better deal with it and get them running fast. At some point, you would have to turn around and head for the barn, and then the race was on. Horses are always in a hurry to get home. It was the best part of the ride. All our barnyard buddies are long gone now, but they all went to heaven as far as we know.

February 2, 2022

5

COME FOR THE VIEW, STAY FOR THE PLASTIC

Something had gone terribly wrong. The morning was ominously silent with no reassuring splatter of raindrops hitting the roof. Searching for answers, I looked out the window and noticed an unnatural brightness in the sky that seemed to intensify with each passing moment. Suddenly, a blinding bright light burst out of the eastern horizon. It was the sun.

You tend to forget about the sun after a couple of months of monsoons. But there it was: a sunny day after months of winter storms. In the old days, that meant one thing. It was time to go to the beach and look for glass balls. These shiny relics of the Asian fishing fleets used to wash up on our shores in great numbers, just waiting for the lucky beachcomber to find them.

That was then. Things have changed. For one thing, there are crowds of people at the beach these days. Encountering these citified beach explorers can be a terrifying experience. Olympic National Park rules for its scenic coastal section require dogs to be on a leash no more than six feet long. Meanwhile, small children are allowed to wander freely. A leash law for children might seem cruel and unusual until you watch a toddler barely able to walk in their oversized rubber boots stumble toward the surf while their unsuspecting parents are busy off in the distance attending to the sanitary requirements of their bathroom-challenged animal companions. These same parents, who would never allow their children to walk out into a busy freeway, think nothing of letting the kids wander into the surf with its freak waves and sucking undertows.

Experienced beachcombers only go to the beach at an outgoing tide to avoid the dreadful experience of being dragged out to sea by an undertow after being pounded into the beach logs by sneaker waves. Modern beachgoers seem to have a total disregard for these concerns. Hoping to avoid a potential tragedy, I continued down the beach, searching for beachcombing treasures hidden in the driftwood. There were no glass balls. There was, however, a dizzying array of plastic of every size and description.

According to the good folks at the American Chemistry Council, we manufacture around 35.4 million tons of plastic every year in the United States alone. Meanwhile, worldwide, we dump billions of pounds of plastic in the ocean every year. There, it forms gigantic floating islands that decay and are eventually absorbed into the pelagic food chain.

Unlike the glass balls, which seem to be increasingly hard to find, plastic is hard to miss. There is no danger of ever running out of plastic because they are constantly making more. Plastic is the wave of the future. It's everywhere we want to be. Where the surf hits the shore, a glittering array of tiny plastics awaits the modern beachcomber. These miniature plastic pieces shine like little colored diamonds in the sand.

It's no wonder fish and other marine life just love to eat pieces of plastic, mistaking them for food. The farther from the surf you go, the bigger the plastic gets. You can find everything from boots to barrels. Sometimes, it's fun to think of where all that plastic came from. It really makes you think it's a small world after all. Picking up plastic may not be as cool as finding glass balls, but it's all we've got left. So, let's all enjoy our wild Pacific coast, where our motto is "come for the view, but stay for the plastic."

February 12, 2020

6

WINTER STEELHEAD

It was daylight on the river. The stars were fading in the cold, gray sky. The river looked like a smoking cauldron of black water oozing through a canyon of frozen rock beneath a tunnel of leaning trees. This caused questions to be asked like, "What on earth am I doing floating down a river in the dark in the darkest days of winter?" The answer was simple enough. Fishing for winter-run steelhead. These have been called the fish of a thousand casts, but no one who fishes for them bothers to count. Sometimes, it's better not to know just how much effort is required to catch a steelhead. Whether it's a thousand casts in the river, a thousand oar strokes on a drift boat, or white-knuckle miles of ice-covered road, people who fish for steelhead just don't seem to care.

In fact, once you start accounting for all the time and effort steelhead fishing demands, it may be time to hang it up and get a life. Real steelhead fishers actually like the nasty weather. They cling to the false hope that freezing temperatures will keep the competition at home where they belong.

Judging from the crowds fishing the West End of the Olympic Peninsula these days, the weather has not been cold enough to make a dent in the hordes of anglers that invade Forks every year at about this time. Some of the locals claim people who fish for steelhead are insane, but compared to what?

Some of my seasonably depressed fancy friends use winter as an excuse to vacation in a tropical paradise. They think that if they can get away from the endless gray of the Pacific Northwest winter, life will be worth living. This is a bad mistake. You still have to come back home from your week in the tropics, then face what's left of the dark and dreary winter with its bills, leaky roofs, and pipes that froze in your absence. As the slush melts into a pond in your basement, you wonder just why you returned from that tropical paradise to a world where it never seems to stop raining.

Meanwhile, someone who just spent the week fishing for steelhead on the constant verge of hypothermia is thrilled with the prospect of a nice, warm rain. It will make the rivers rise and bring in more fish. What if we have another nasty Canadian cold snap on the way? That's great news to anyone who fishes for steelhead. It will make the rivers drop back into perfect shape. All weather is good weather for those who delude themselves into steelhead fishing. Many of them have grown an extra layer of fur and blubber as a physical adaptation to the arctic conditions of winter fishing. Some fishermen even claim they have heated drift boats. Anyone who says that is either a liar, a guide, or both. An open drift boat is impossible to heat.

Boat heaters can be tricky. Usually about the time you feel your feet starting to thaw out in front of the heater, your boots are on fire. This can be a bad time to hook a fish. A silver torpedo of a fish jumps out of the river. People start screaming at you. You try to reel in the fish with icy fingers in frozen mittens that accidently push the reel's free spool button, causing a huge bird's nest of tangled line that breaks with a crack like a pistol shot as the fish heads downriver. You sit in a cloud of burning rubber smoke and can barely wait for it to happen again.

February 15, 2011

13

7

THE SECRET LURE

If I said it once I said it a million times: I need another secret lure like I need a hole in the head. Don't get me wrong. Secret lures can be the secret to good fishing. Trouble is, the effectiveness of secret lures can be time sensitive, depending upon run timing, clarity of the water, and the number of people using the secret lure. That can make it not a secret anymore. Typically, about the time you find a secret lure, it will stop catching fish and you will have to find another one.

It can be a very frustrating experience to shop for a secret lure in a tackle store. That's because in any display of fishing lures, there are the empty spaces that indicate certain items have sold out. Those were the lures that caught fish, the ones you wanted to buy, the ones that aren't there. You can ask if they'll sell you the lures that aren't there, but chances are all you'll get is attitude.

The best way to get a secret lure is to find one on the water where it was fished. One day, I noticed a funny-colored plug floating down the middle of a smooth stretch of river. Then, I saw a large boil and a silver flash of a steelhead just underneath the lure! If a fish would bite at a lure floating on the surface, I wondered if it would work on the bottom of the river. It did. That lure caught fish until the paint was eaten off it. It kept catching fish, even after it was chewed down to bare plastic. It didn't matter what color the plug was. It must have been the action or the shape of it the fish liked. Sometimes, the secret of a secret lure remains unknown.

The secret lures you find generally share several identifying features, such as bent hooks, scratched paint, and maybe some broken line still attached. These are clues the lure was badly abused. That's the one you're looking for. Plugs and bobbers can be found where they washed into back eddies with the flotsam. Sinking lures are generally on the bottom of the river, which can make them tougher to get. The rewards can be great. A root-wad stuck in a good fishing hole can snag enough lures to start a tackle store. Retrieving this treasure trove is not without its hazards. Just ask the guy who hooked the winch on the front of his pickup to the small end of a gear-grabbing snag in the Hoh River. This was back before this sort of thing was illegal. Things went OK at first. Then, the big end of the snag caught the current and started dragging the truck toward the setting sun, sideways.

It might be safer to look for secret lures in some of the tree branches overhanging our more popular fishing holes. There are so many spinners, spoons, jigs, floats, and colored lines in the trees, it looks like they were decorated for Christmas. Folks suggested I prune the limbs to get the lures back. They forgot I do all my tree pruning with a shotgun and with the price of shells these days, no way.

No doubt the best way to find a new secret lure is to get it out of the mouth of a fish that you caught. You may have to catch many hundreds of steelhead to find a secret lure with this method, but nobody said it was easy.

February 20, 2011

MORE RESEARCH IS NEEDED

It was another tough week in the news. Steelhead fishing on the Olympic Peninsula has gotten so crowded you'll want to bring your own rock to stand on if you hope to make a cast. The Washington Department of Fish and Wildlife closed almost every other river in the state to even catch-and-release fishing, while the rivers of the Peninsula were left open. This crowded the last remaining hardcore steelhead anglers from all over the United States and beyond into smaller and smaller areas where they could be studied and monitored with a helicopter, drones, and trail cams. Teams of fish checkers, surveyors, and fish cops patrolled up and down the river and interrogated anglers. Add to this a series of the most complicated fishing regulations ever invented. The Hoh, a river just over fifty miles long, is divided into eight sections, each with its own seasons and gear restrictions. Some allow you to fish out of a floating device (a.k.a., a boat) on certain days of the week, but not others.

My solution to these bizarre rules was to take the plug out of my boat. It would not be a floating device. It would be a sinking device. While no one in their right mind would get in a sinking boat to go on a winter steelhead fishing trip, if I only guided people who were in their right minds, I would seldom be employed.

The idea that people who fish for steelhead are insane is not a new one. How else could you explain someone spending thousands of dollars traveling thousands of miles to slowly freeze to death trying to catch a fish that, on any given day, may or may not actually exist.

We should have known. Once the state studied steelhead anglers, it would only be a matter of time before they were as endangered as the fish we were trying to catch. It may be just a coincidence, but every other creature that the state of Washington is "studying," from the marbled murrelet to the spotted owl, the southern resident orca, the mountain goats, and even our iconic Olympic marmots, have had their populations decline or disappear altogether while they were being studied.

As more and more anglers were confined into a smaller area by the scientists, the overcrowding led to disputes over fish and other antisocial behaviors. This led to the row versus wade dispute. Wading anglers, who were stomping steelhead eggs into the gravel where the steelhead were spawning, wanted to ban boat anglers to keep them from dragging their anchors through the same gravel. The overcrowding of anglers led to dangerous incidents. Anglers flipped their boats in desperate attempts to fish rivers they were not capable of rowing. The lucky ones were rescued. Others were not.

Meanwhile, scientists have long studied the effects of overcrowding on mice and rats in the laboratory. The results give us a chilling perspective on human behavior. Back in the 1960s, a researcher named John Calhoun created a rat utopia and a mouse paradise with abundant food, where the rodents were free to overpopulate. This quickly led to overcrowding, disputes over available food, and seemingly sinister antisocial behavior that Calhoun termed "behavioral sinks." Over time, the surviving rodents displayed a lack of interest in sex and raising their young. While Calhoun's research is still being debated, one can't help but wonder if humans would behave in the same way, given the same conditions.

A striking parallel to Calhoun's experiment was observed among steelhead anglers on our Olympic Peninsula rivers last winter. Once described as a fishing paradise and a steelhead utopia with abundant fish, the increased crowding of anglers into the study area led to disputes over available fish. The effects of the experiment were reflected in the demographics of the surviving anglers on our rivers, where very few females and almost no juveniles were observed fishing for steelhead. This could indicate that the overcrowded anglers, like the overcrowded rats, had lost interest in sex and raising their young. Whether this represents a behavioral sink or an evolutionary trend is unclear. More research is needed.

March 2, 2022

9

A NEW STATE FLOWER

Thank you for reading this. Sometimes, I think that if you didn't read this, no one would. You can count on me to expose the cutting-edge issues that make this country so cool. For too long, we have been forced to ignore an issue that is at the center of our quality of life here in the great state of Washington. Should we be forced to ignore our history, which has made this country what it is today? I, and a lot of other right-thinking Washingtonians, don't think so. It is time we address a past miscarriage of justice that should not be allowed to continue.

It is our fervent hope that once you consider the facts, you will agree that our state flower, the coast rhododendron, hides a dirty little secret. The rhododendron does not occur east of the Cascade Mountains. It is, in fact, an invasive species to many of the citizens it supposedly represents. This contemptible form of botanical regionalism has no place in a free and open society, where we should all have the opportunity to celebrate a flower whose cultural and historic significance celebrates our past while issuing a warning about our future.

All of this makes the rhododendron totally unqualified for this high office when compared to what should be our true state flower: the skunk cabbage. Also known as *Lysichitum americanus*, it was called "Uncle" by Native Americans in the time before salmon. Back then, the skunk cabbage was considered a starvation food. That was after the melting of the continental ice sheet about fifteen thousand years ago. It took the salmon about six thousand years to colonize our rivers. Our evergreen forests had yet to be established. With no salmon in our rivers and no forests on our land, things were tough all over. This was long before there was a Washington Department of Fish and Wildlife to blame.

The legend says when the first spring salmon swam upriver, Uncle Skunk Cabbage told them he had kept the people from starving. As a reward, the salmon gave the skunk cabbage a war club, an elk-hide blanket, and rich soil along the river, where they live to this day.

All of this serves as a warning: If we manage our salmon to extinction, we could go back to eating skunk cabbage. Even after the coming of the salmon, the skunk cabbage provided the people with medicines that treated everything from headaches and fevers to female troubles. The leaves were used to store cakes of dried berries before the invention of Tupperware.

Compare this legend with the story of the rhododendron. It was discovered in 1792 by Archibald Menzies when he and British Captain George Vancouver landed at Discovery Bay. The United States had just fought a Revolutionary War with the British and were about to fight another one in 1812. Our founding fathers would never have allowed a shrub discovered by the British to become a state flower, so why should we?

The luxuriant, yellow blossoms of the skunk cabbage can be irresistible to tourists. When you see people picking bouquets of skunk cabbage flowers, you know they are from somewhere else. While picking wildflowers is generally discouraged, our tourist visitors can pick all the skunk cabbage flowers they want—even if they do throw them out the window as soon as the skunky aroma pervades their vehicle.

All of this begs the question: Should Washington be represented by a scraggly little shrub? Or a majestic flower that represents our history and culture? You decide.

March 20, 2024

10

A BIRD-WATCHING GUIDE

Daylight on the river comes mighty early these days. It is a peaceful time of day to watch the stars fade away as the sunrise glows across the mountains. I like to listen to the silence of the wilderness. Silence is one of the rarest things on earth. Unfortunately, silence can be very brief in the wilderness. Then, there is the pinging call of the boreal owl. It sounds like someone beating a metal wedge that's stuck in a round of firewood. There is the low hooting of the great horned owl that sounds like a drunk person trying to imitate a foghorn. Once the owls stop calling, it's only a matter of time until a murder of crows flies out of its roost like a cawing black amoeba in the clouds. This evil portent always seems to wake up the woodpeckers.

The pileated woodpecker is a red-crested forest pest about the size of a crow. This is a normally shy bird that spends its time jack-hammering massive holes in dry snags in search of bugs. The woodpeckers perform a wilderness public service that rids the forest of insects and provides nesting cavities for other birds—until their mating season, when the woodpeckers begin a destructive practice of drumming on dry wood. This can be an old snag, a telephone pole, or wood-paneled dream home. All the while, they shriek an obnoxious call that sounds like a house cat with its tail caught in the door. The woodpeckers repeat this performance for hours each day for weeks on end until the baby woodpeckers hatch. These baby woodpeckers can make even more noise with their constant demands for food.

Meanwhile, on the forest floor, other birds are making even more noise. The winter wren, though tiny, makes up for its small size with a long-winded call that can be loud enough to require hearing protection for us sensitive types. The song of the winter wren is not the bubbly symphony of nature you might think. The latest scientific research suggests that like most birds, the winter wren is engaged in a vicious form of trash-talking other wrens, in an effort to win mates, establish a territory, and defend the nest.

The winter wrens may be offensive, but at least they do not gather in flocks. The pine siskin is a drab little bird with a dismal little call that flits about in huge flocks and eats the seeds of trees. These tiny birds are easily frightened by almost anything. As is typical with most birds, they tend to have a bowel movement when they are alarmed. It lessens the payload on takeoff. Finding yourself under an alarmed flock of siskins can be a queasy nature experience. You might think it is raining, but it is not. Don't look up.

While watching birds in the rainforest can be a pointless exercise in frustration and disgust, watching birds on the river can be even worse than that. The water ouzel, or dipper, is a small, drab, gray bird about the size of a tennis ball with the unique ability to walk underwater. The rest of the time, they stand on the rocks and bob up and down like they are about to have a seizure, while yammering away with a bothersome twitter that always seems to get on my nerves. As the days lengthen, the baby salmonids begin their migration to the sea. This triggers a migration of saw-billed mergansers upriver to eat what is left of our endangered fisheries. All of this could force me to become a bird-watching guide.

March 24, 2010

11

THE CHEMICAL BARRAGE

They say public speaking is one of the greatest fears a human being can face. Fortunately, these days there is an audio-visual aid that makes this odious chore more enjoyable. If there is one thing I would need at a public speaking event besides a gun to my head, it would be a laser pointer. A laser pointer by itself is not an evil thing. You'd never guess that these pen-sized mini-lasers are the greatest single crowd control tool since the invention of the water cannon, if used properly. I went to a presentation about the battle against invasive plants hosted by the University of Washington School of Forestry at their palatial digs in the high-rent district above uptown Forks. If you ever wonder where your tax dollars went, get a load of this place. It has a futuristic vibe that would make it a great location for a sci-fi movie.

It is the home of the ribbon stringers. Those are people who string colored plastic ribbons through the forests and streams of the Olympic Peninsula to prove they've been there. It is illegal to point a laser at an airplane pilot. It blinds people and distracts them. It is somehow perfectly acceptable to point a laser pointer at a screen during a slide show and shake it around faster than the human eye can follow. After a minute or so of trying to follow the laser across the screen, the visual senses are in shock. After an hour and a half of being subjected to the laser pointer, I was almost willing to believe glyphosate was as harmless as the people who make the stuff say it is. Glyphosate is the latest magic bullet in the chemical battle against weeds that began with 2,4-d. In her 1962 book *Silent Spring,* Rachel Carson wrote about the effects DDT, 2,4-d, and 2,4,5-T on the environment. On the Olympic Peninsula, 2,4-d was sprayed along power lines to keep the lines clear. It was sprayed on clear cuts to kill the red alder and anything else that would interfere with the Douglas fir seedlings. Industry experts assured us it was merely a harmless salt that just dried up and disappeared. We were told we could drink the stuff, which was good news since it was sprayed in every watershed on the Olympic Peninsula. So, it was a surprise to learn that fifty years later, the alder trees are worth more than the Douglas fir and 2,4-d is not as harmless as the experts assured us.

It was a key ingredient in Agent Orange, whose effects on returning Vietnam veterans was finally recognized by the US government after years of human suffering. To understand science, you have to know who is paying the scientist. Since then, the chemical industry has invented new "harmless" chemicals and reasons for spraying them. Currently, glyphosate is being sprayed along our rivers as an excuse for salmon restoration. Again, we are told this herbicide just a harmless salt. Historically, fish, birds, bees, and humans have to sicken and die from the chemical barrage before it can be proven beyond a shadow of a doubt that it is harmful and we stop using them. I sincerely hope the latest harmless herbicide isn't as harmful as the last batch we were dosed with. Rachel Carson called herbicides "as crude a weapon as any cave man's club, the chemical barrage has been hurled against the fabric of life." She didn't need a laser pointer.

March 26, 2016

12

THE VOYAGE OF THE *LYDIA*

The Corps of Discovery was in trouble. On November 5, 1805, they had reached the ocean after their journey across the continent to camp on the stormy northern shore at the mouth of the Columbia River. Exposed to the violence of the southwest gales pushing huge waves that flooded their camp, the expedition decided to move to a more sheltered spot. Though this was a military expedition, the captains, Lewis and Clark, decided to hold an election to let everyone decide if they should stay put, move upriver to the falls of the Columbia, or move across the river to the southern shore. This represented the first election in the Pacific Northwest where everyone, including the black slave York and the Shoshone woman Sacagawea, voted.

On December 7, the expedition found an elevated spot on the southern shore of the Columbia that was thirty feet above the high tide. They began making shelters and a palisade. There were plenty of elk in the area. The expedition set up a salt-making operation on the ocean beach. After the soggy winter of 1806 at Fort Clatsop, they prepared to paddle their canoes back up the flooding Columbia River in late March, with nothing more than a handful of trade goods that could be carried in "two handkerchiefs."

Fortunately, during the winter, they had made three hundred or four hundred pairs of elk-hide moccasins. Captain Clark had sealed their remaining 140 pounds of gunpowder inside waterproof lead canisters so they had plenty of ammunition. However, Captain Lewis lamented the fact that President Jefferson hadn't sent a ship to rescue or supply the expedition at the mouth of the Columbia. All winter, they had subsisted on lean elk meat while trying to trade for food with the hard-bargaining Columbia River tribes. Among them were the Chinook, who already had experience in the sea otter trade.

In 1778, Captain Cook had sailed past our coast, then known as New Albion. Cook had missed the Strait of Juan de Fuca in the fog, naming Cape Flattery as an historic insult to the navigator for whom the then-imaginary strait was named. Captain Cook proceeded to Vancouver Island, where by chance he traded with the Nootka People for twenty sea otter skins that were worth $800 in China. In 1785, Captain James Hanna visited Nootka Sound, trading iron bars for 546 sea otter skins worth $20,600 in China. The rush was on. Hanna was soon followed by the American captain Robert Gray, who first entered the mouth of the Columbia on May 11, 1792, slaughtering a canoe-load of Indians with cannon fire on the way.

Gray was soon followed by a number of ships from Boston and Bristol engaged in the sea otter trade. This was a global enterprise, where sea captains traded on the Northwest coast for furs. These were traded in Canton for silk, tea, porcelain, and cloth that was traded back to Boston or Bristol. The Indians called Americans "Bostons" and the British "King George men," both of which were called "cloth men" because that's some of what they traded. Lewis and Clark observed Indians along the Columbia dressed in sailor's clothing and cursing like sailors who claimed ships entered the mouth of the river every spring to trade for furs.

This caused questions to be asked. With all the American ships trading on the Northwest coast between 1792 and 1806, why didn't President Jefferson send a ship to rescue or resupply the Corps of Discovery after their harrowing journey across the continent? There are several plausible reasons for this perceived oversight. It could be because Jefferson had no way of knowing where on the west coast of the continent the Corps of Discovery would emerge or if the expedition had even survived. Even if England didn't care about an American rescue ship, Spain considered the Pacific Ocean a Spanish lake. President Jefferson didn't want to risk offending them with what would have been a risky venture at the time.

In an ironic twist of historical fate, unknown to Lewis and Clark at the time, a fortnight after they had abandoned Fort Clatsop on the southern shore to return eastward across the continent, the American brigantine *Lydia* under Captain Samuel Hill anchored up on the north shore and began cutting spars to repair the ship.

Lewis and Clark had given a letter to the Chinook Chief Delashelwilt to give to any ship he encountered describing the "kindness and attention" they had received from the Indians. In addition, it described their outward journey across the continent and their return route. The Indians gave Captain Hill of the *Lydia* the letter and told him the expedition had just been there two weeks before and all were in good health and spirits. Eventually, Captain Hill delivered the letter to Boston by way of Canton.

Coincidentally, the Englishmen John Jewitt and John Thompson were aboard the *Lydia*. Jewitt and Thompson had been rescued by the *Lydia* after being held captive for two years by Maquinna, chief of the Nootka on Vancouver Island. Maquinna had a long history of dealing with Europeans. During his visit to Nootka in 1785, John Hanna had invited Maquinna aboard his ship, the *Sea Otter*. Maquinna was given a chair above a pile of gunpowder and told this was an honor the English gave chiefs. Thinking it was dark sand, Maquinna sat in the chair while a sailor lit the charge, blowing the chief up into the air and burning his back side. When someone stole a chisel from the *Sea Otter*, Hanna retaliated by firing a cannon on a canoe full of Indians, killing twenty men, women, and children, including several chiefs.

Another trader entered Maquinna's house, scared his nine wives, and stole forty of his best sea otter skins. The Spanish commander Estaban Martinez killed Maquinna's friend and fellow Nootka chief Callicum. All of this convinced Maquinna to take his revenge on the next European ship he encountered.

That occurred in 1803, when Captain John Salter of the trading ship *Boston* insulted Maquinna over a broken lock on a shotgun. Maquinna took the ship, killing everyone aboard but John Thompson the sailmaker and the blacksmith John Jewitt. Eventually, John Jewitt got a written message to Yutramaki, a Makah chief, who gave it to Captain Samuel Hill of the *Lydia*, who took Maquinna hostage to gain the Englishmen's release in 1805.

The story of the *Lydia* and Yutramaki does not end there. The *Lydia*, with Captain T. Brown as master, rescued the survivors of the Russian ship *Sv. Nikolai* at Neah Bay in the spring of 1810. The *Sv. Nikolai* had wrecked just north of LaPush in November 1808. The twenty-two shipwreck survivors fled south in a running battle with the Quileute.

Anna Petrovna, the wife of Captain Bulygin of the *Nikolai* and the first European woman on the Olympic Peninsula, was kidnapped by members of the Hoh tribe, who were ferrying the Russians across the Hoh River in canoes. After a running battle, the other survivors spent the winter on the upper Hoh. Eventually, the Russians acquired canoes to float down the river in a desperate attempt to make it out to Destruction Island, where a passing ship might rescue them.

Near the mouth of the Hoh, Captain Bulygin tried to ransom his wife Anna Petrovna from her captors. Anna told her husband she was staying with the Indians under the protection of Yutramaki. This was the same Yutramaki, the Makah chief, who had rescued the captives from Maquinna at Nootka Sound. Anna Petrovna said he was "an upright and virtuous man" who had rendered many services to her, would protect the Russians, and would contact two ships that were known to be transiting the Strait of Juan de Fuca for their eventual rescue. Some of the Russians surrendered. The rest were captured by the Hoh people.

Yutramaki negotiated the ransom and release of thirteen of the *Nikolai* survivors who had been scattered from the Columbia River to Neah Bay. Anna Petrovna was not among them. All of this begs the question: Was this ship the same *Lydia* that had rescued the survivors of the *Boston*, narrowly missed the Corps of Discovery, and later rescued the survivors of the *Sv. Nikolai*? Or was the *Lydia* the name of a number of vessels trading along the coast at the time? Those who ignore history will never know.

March 30, 2022

13

A SHORT HISTORY OF FISHING LAWS

We're exploring a bizarre bit of bureaucratic bungling. The state of Washington demands that we purchase our new fishing licenses on April 1 but does not come out with the fishing laws until the fourth of July. Fishing violations can involve fines of up to $5,000, forfeiture of fishing gear, fishing boat, and the truck you used to tow all that stuff around, and a criminal record. Consequently, many people have simply quit fishing in Washington altogether because it's too complicated, expensive, and downright dangerous.

Who could blame them? The fishing laws in Washington are so complicated that almost no one can understand them. This was not always the case. The kings of England and Scotland started making fishing laws back in the Middle Ages. Generally speaking, fishing was much better in the Middle Ages than it is today. The fishing laws were much simpler, although violations could involve a more severe punishment. For example, in 1318, Robert the Bruce, King of Scotland, declared that a person convicted of poaching salmon on a royal estate for the second time could be put to death. King Edward III of England made it illegal to use salmon for pig feed. In the 1100s, Richard the Lionheart may have come up with our oldest fishing law. During the Lionheart's reign, described by some historians as an "orgy of medieval savagery," it became illegal to block a salmon stream.

Flash forward to our modern world, where we have spent the last century building dams with no fish passage in our state. The Washington Department of Fish and Wildlife estimates there are more than 19,000 barriers stopping fish passage. Of these, there are approximately 2,000 culverts that impede fish. In 2001, the Treaty Tribes of Washington sued the state of Washington over their culverts that were blocking 1,000 miles of streams. Ultimately, they won a US Supreme Court case in 2018, giving Washington until 2030 to fix their culverts.

That is happening now with the passage of the Infrastructure, Investments, and Jobs Act of 2021 that provides up to five billion dollars for a nationwide effort to eliminate fish passage barriers. These are defined as anything that hinders fish from moving upstream or down. That could include a dam, culvert, or smolt trap.

Every spring, our streams are blocked by smolt traps that catch young salmon and steelhead migrating downstream out to sea. Smolt traps can be a valid method of gathering data but not if they block the entire stream. In the spring, steelhead and sea-run cutthroat migrate up our creeks to spawn, but they can't if the stream is blocked by a smolt trap. When fish are stuck below a smolt trap, they are vulnerable to a wide variety of predators, including people who know that fishing at a smolt trap can be awesome. Steelhead that migrated upstream before the smolt trap was installed can't get back downstream once the smolt trap blocks the creek. Steelhead do not die like the salmon after they spawn. Steelhead go back downstream to the ocean so they can come back and spawn again, unless there's a smolt trap. Fishing above a fish trap can be awesome.

Meanwhile, the young salmon, steelhead, and cutthroat caught in the traps are in danger of floods, predators, and rough handling during the most vulnerable time in their lives, when they miraculously transition from fresh to salt water. Where's Richard the Lionheart when you need him?

April 13, 2022

14

THE FIRST SALMON

The blooming of the salmonberries marks a change in the season. In the old days, these blossoms signaled the beginning of the spring Chinook run up the rivers. It's called the first salmon because they're the first to swim upriver in the spring. They do not spawn until late summer or fall. They survive on their body fat, making their flesh rich and succulent. Salmon oil is beneficial for heart health and brain function. Just think how much more intelligent this story would be if I could just catch a springer. But I digress.

The salmon kept people alive since they colonized our rivers after the ice age. People believed salmon came from a big house at the bottom of the ocean where they lived in human form. When it was time to run upriver, they put on salmon robes and voluntarily sacrificed their bodies for the benefit of humans and everything on the river from the tiniest insects to the tallest trees. Then, the spirit of the salmon would return to their ocean house. The first salmon caught in the spring was treated as a special guest. The meat was shared. The heart and bones of the first salmon were washed and returned to the river. Care was taken so no dogs could get a piece of the first salmon.

On April 19, 1806, the Lewis and Clark expedition dropped by a first salmon ceremony at the Dalles on the Columbia River. Captain Clark observed, "The whole village was rejoicing today over having caught a single salmon, which was considered as the harbinger of vast quantities in four or five days. In order to hasten their arrival, the Indians, according to custom, dressed the fish and cut it into small pieces, one of which was given to every child in the village."

It was believed as long as the salmon were treated with respect, the fish would run forever.

Instead, we began the commercial exploitation of salmon. In 1834, Nathanial Wyeth hatched a scheme to ship barrels of salted salmon from the Columbia River to Hawaii and the East Coast.

James Swan described the salmon fishing in Shoalwater, now Willapa Bay, in June of 1852. There, he and his Chinook Indian friends caught a hundred Chinook salmon weighing up to seventy-eight pounds with a single haul of a spruce-root seine net. These fish, called "June hogs" for their size and fat content, were doomed to extinction. In 1867, the first of many salmon canneries was built on the Columbia River. By 1878, cannery operators were facing a shortage of spring Chinook. They built the first fish hatchery.

By 1881, there were thirty canneries employing 2,500 to 3,000 mostly Scandinavian fisherman while 4,000 Chinese cut the fish to fit into cans. Every form of net was used to choke the Columbia from one bank to another, making it difficult for salmon to swim upriver. Fish wheels pumped 20,000 to 50,000 fish a day out of the river until Washington outlawed them in 1935.

By then, they were building the Grand Coulee Dam on the Columbia River. It had no fish ladders, ending the salmon run into British Columbia. Eventually, sixty dams were built in the Columbia basin. Since then, the Columbia River has served as a road map to extinction on other rivers. By the new millennium, an increasing human population with exploding pinniped and predatory bird populations has resulted in salmon going extinct in 40 percent of their historic range in the Pacific Northwest. Nineteen populations of salmon and steelhead are listed as threatened under the Endangered Species Act.

This proves the belief that if we disrespect the salmon, they will not run forever.

April 17, 2024

15

THE NEW GOLD RUSH

They say America is a country divided and exploited by plundering gangs of panty-grabbing politicians eternally enthroned by an apathetic population of unregistered voters who get their fake news from a drive-by lap dog media. I say if it isn't fixed, don't break it. We should stand up for what's right with America. Instead of boo-hooing unsolvable problems we can't afford to fix, we should look to our storied past to visualize our sustainable future. We should remember our pioneer forebears who journeyed from sea to shining sea as an experiment in democracy. When viewed through the lens of history, today's current events are no mystery. It's all been done before.

Colonel James S. Coolican was a visionary promoter with a keen business sense. He served as president of the Port Angeles Board of Trade and the Clallam County Immigrants Association. By immigrants, Col. Coolican did not mean the Chinese. They were accused of taking jobs from Americans and smuggling opium. The colonel wanted a "desirable class of immigrants:" northern Europeans along with any Englishman who cared to jump ship, and, of course, women to swamp out and cook in the logging camps. We didn't celebrate diversity back in 1897.

Col. Coolican wrote about the "good time coming" in his promotional pamphlet "Port Angeles, the Gate City of the Pacific Coast." The colonel said that "veins of precious metals, ores and coal bulge out of the hillside." Gold Creek, Silver Lake, and Oil City were named for the treasures soon to be found. Col. Coolican raised $10,000 from the locals to buy a genuine diamond drill and followed his coal mining dreams up Tumwater Creek. The colonel drilled six hundred feet and found nothing but sand and gravel, which were readily available at the surface. Except for some manganese, the Olympic Peninsula was never much of a mining district—until now.

As president of the Oil City Economic Development Council, I was hunting for government grants to lessen America's dependence of foreign energy sources by drilling for oil in Oil City. Failing that, I found another source of mineral wealth that's been hiding in plain sight for years. It's like the old log trucker said: "For every mile of road there are two miles of ditch." These days, the ditches are filled to overflowing with a promising source of mineral wealth contained in the inexhaustible piles of empty cans and bottles that are now worth ten cents apiece in Oregon. While other forms of mining are burdened with obsessive government regulation, mining cans and bottles out of our ditches is under the regulatory radar.

Researchers retraced the resurgence of refuse to a migration of fishermen from all over the country and around the world. When their practices were outlawed by civilized societies elsewhere, these fishing refugees came to the Olympic Peninsula, where they were accused of taking fish away from the locals. I'm not saying all the immigrant fishermen are litterbugs, but it seems like all the litterbugs fish here. Maybe it's just a coincidence their colorful spoor appeared at the start of fishing season. However, researchers identified the genetic traits of the immigrant fisherman's garbage by analyzing the sudden appearance of Lite beer cans, chip sacks, and empty "chew" containers shortly after fishing season opened.

I'm sure fishermen don't consider tossing garbage in the wilderness as nothing more than leaving a piece of themselves for the rest of us to enjoy. Who cares? It's like Colonel Coolican said: "There's a good time coming." Anyone with rubber gloves and a garbage sack can strike it rich in just a short section of ditch.

April 19, 2017

16

THE NEW POLLUTION

I've been feeling a little weird lately, but I'm not going to waste valuable print space falling into the typical wilderness gossip columnist trap of going on about my medical problems. Maybe I'm just down because of all the new catch and release fishing regulations. I haven't been able to club a fish lately. That used to make me feel better. My psychiatrist said it was a transference thing, so I punched him. Sorry to be so emotional. It's just that I've been having these violent mood swings from omnipotent paranoia to gut-wrenching depression. I'm sure it's just the male menopause talking. I started crying while watching a car commercial. I could have sworn I was experiencing some bloating, dizziness, and other side effects that told me that I've been eating way too much fish lately.

I started noticing these symptoms shortly after a recent news article described the 97,000 pounds of drugs, hormones, and personal care product residues that are pumped into the water every year by 106 publicly owned wastewater treatment plants in Puget Sound. The chemicals are not monitored, regulated, or removed from wastewater.

A landmark study by NOAA scientists found an alphabet soup of chemical residues in the tissues of young salmon that had to swim through Puget Sound. That could explain why these young fish have such a hard time migrating out to the big world and becoming adults. Experiments with juvenile human offspring have shown that exposure to these chemicals, including nicotine, caffeine, OxyContin,

Paxil, Valium, Zoloft, and cocaine, can produce the same results. These substances are called "chemicals of concern" since their effects on fish and human growth, behavior, reproduction, and immune function remain unknown.

We don't know what levels these chemicals are present in adult fish. We don't know the effect on marine mammals who eat fish, but those at the top of the food chain, like humans, would be the most vulnerable. The side effects of chemical experiments on self-medicating human subjects are well documented, producing a myriad of antisocial, evolutionary dead-end behaviors from raiding the fridge to robbing the liquor store. The potential dangers of a "coked up" killer whale looking for more, a tweaker seal strung out on meth, or a thousand-pound sea lion on an OxyContin binge should be fairly obvious to everyone by now.

Still, there could be a bright side to the new pollution. Over the years, I have used just about every excuse there is for not catching a fish, from the sun being in my eyes to forgetting my medication. Nowadays, the reasons for not catching a fish are obvious. How else can you possibly explain fish jumping all around and you're not catching one? The fish are on drugs!

This new pollution has been discovered while the Department of Ecology is attempting to determine the exact amount of seafood each Washington citizen consumes in a year. That's to set pollution levels for business and industry to meet before they affect human health. Relying on humans to say what they eat is risky. As the NOAA study data indicates, many of the humans are on drugs, so how are they supposed to remember what or if they ate? How many times have you asked who ate the last cookie or all the ice cream? There is no reply.

With the new pollution, it could be only a matter of time before fish come with labels warning you to not be pregnant or run heavy equipment when you eat them. I don't know. It could be the chemicals talking.

April 22, 2017

17

SPRINGTIME ON THE RANCH

It's springtime on the ranch. The grass is growing. It's time to stop feeding hay despite what the inmates say. I never set out to be a cowboy, just trying to help a neighbor. I know from hard personal experience just how dangerous this profession can be. It's been said that if you lift a calf every day, you will become the strongest man on earth. I don't know about that. All I know is if you feed a calf every day from birth and raise it like a puppy, giving it head-butting lessons, it can eventually become a ton of fun charging across the pasture to play.

Everyone knows a cowboy has to be able to ride a horse to do the job. Not having a horse in the early days might have been a roadblock in my career if I had not stumbled upon the idea of riding cows instead. When hopping upon a razor-backed dairy steer, it helps if the animal is asleep. This generally caused the critter to bolt upward like a ballistic missile and the rodeo was on.

Eventually, I gave up riding cows and spent a lot of time searching for them. Among all the cows in the general vicinity, a certain percentage of fence jumpers kept us busy looking for them. Cows are scary. Anything that weighs half a ton is scary, especially if it is hungry and described by the owner as "frisky." There could be many reasons for the cows being rambunctious. Cows are a lot like humans. Despite being given all the food they could possibly eat, they'll fight over it. I did not want to be involved in the race for who got the first bale. I was just the new guy trying to please everyone at once.

Then, tragedy struck. A cow died during calving season. The cows held a funeral. They all stood around in a circle and mooed. It was very touching. I thought the coyotes or the bears coming out of hibernation would be drawn to the carcass and threaten the calves, but no worries. The cows would not let a crow land in the field, so a coyote or a bear did not stand a chance.

Inevitably, I was late with the feed. I blamed it on my fishing problem. I showed up, eventually. The cows were not amused. They stood bellowing as I loaded the truck until it was half full, then walked across the field to where they would be fed. That meant I had little time to load the truck and get to the field before the cows arrived. I didn't make it. Once inside the field, I felt the truck lurch sideways like the bridge of the starship *Enterprise* being hit with a tractor beam. Driving through a field of cows is a lot like driving on a freeway with humans. They tailgate and don't signal much. I attempted to outrun the cows by gunning the truck up to almost five miles an hour, forgetting they can sprint about thirty miles an hour on the straightaway. I felt the thud of bales being ripped from the truck by the hungry cows. That was bad. They might ingest the bale strings that could get stuck in their gizzards. I jumped from the truck with my imaginary light saber, a four-foot length of white plastic pipe. By waving my saber and reciting Shakespeare, I retrieved the baling twine. It was good to be alive.

April 26, 2015

18

THE BEST ARBOR DAY EVER

How was your Arbor Day? Traditionally celebrated on the last Friday in April, Arbor Day is probably the most significant holiday you've never heard of, so it's not a surprise you missed it. Arbor Day is the favorite holiday for those who loathe holidays. It's free of the emotional baggage of other holidays that plunge us into an orgy of consumer debt, social anxiety, and holiday travel and have us ask, "Why can't Arbor Day last all year?"

All you have to do to celebrate Arbor Day in the traditional manner is plant a tree. It will grow. Keep planting trees and you'll have a forest. Experts contend the practice of sitting in a forest, called forest bathing, is an uplifting experience. It acts as an antidote to the stress of our modern lives by bringing our vibrational patterns into a healing alignment. It's believed the forest facilitates the cleansing of all our stored-up negativity, stress, and psychotic episodes, allowing them to be absorbed into the ecosystem by reinforcing the idea that we are one with nature.

Recent scientific data indicates trees might possibly improve many health issues, such as mental illness, ADHD, and depression. Some believe trees can alleviate headaches, improve reaction time, and enhance concentration levels. Other imagined benefits of forest bathing include a greater life expectancy, a higher sense of meaningfulness, lower cognitive anxiety, and better body image. But is that fair to the trees? Everything is offensive if you think about it and I have.

Trees are not just used for our houses, furniture, and paper products anymore. These days, trees are a psychic dumping ground for all of our personal problems. Inevitably, forest bathing devolved into an abusive scenario of unwanted touching, known as tree hugging.

Recently, some scientists somewhere speculated trees communicate their needs and send each other nutrients through an elaborate, symbiotic relationship with the mycelium of fungi buried in the soil, similar to neural networks in human brains. Trees talk to each other, sending warning signals about environmental change and death. Research has not revealed the trees' emotional response to an invasion of tree huggers.

To the trees, the human race most likely represents a bunch of road building, carbon spewing apes with fire and chainsaws whose daily activities push the Earth closer to midnight on the doomsday clock. That's not something trees want to hug.

Then, there's the physical harm abusive tree hugging can cause. People weigh a whole lot more than they used to. A tree subjected to an abusive "group hug" can be devastated. While hugging the tree, you're stomping the filigree of fungi mycelium beneath the soil that not only feeds the tree but sequesters carbon from the atmosphere. Abusive tree hugging can remove the rich tapestry of moss, lichen, and liverworts covering the bark. These preserve moisture and provide a home to bacteria that take nitrogen from the air and supply it to the tree so it can grow still larger. It's easy to identify trees that have been victims of tree hugging. The soil around their trunks has been stomped into a muddy patch where nothing grows. Their bark is bereft of the forest community that grows on trees that have not been subjected to this unwanted touching.

It is hoped that this Arbor Day, people will stop exploitation of our forests by venting their personal problems with the questionable practice of forest bathing. Really, the trees don't want to hear it. It's time to stop abusive tree hugging worldwide. Stop crushing the liverworts. Hug a human instead and have the best Arbor Day ever!

May 1, 2024

19

THE SEVEN STAGES OF DEVICE DEPRIVATION

On some of these clear spring days, you just know summer is on the way. Maybe it's the seasonally adjusted gas prices that tell you it's only a matter of time before the tourist hordes invade the Olympic Peninsula. With the miracle of climate change, people down south (we call them "climate refugees") are busy planning trips away from their homes where summertime temperatures get over a hundred or so degrees for weeks on end.

While the locals will complain about a wet, rainy summer, it's perfect for the climate refugees who have come north precisely for the cool weather. They think being wet is cool and who am I, a concierge of the tourist industry, to argue. Unfortunately, this dream vacation is often marred by a yawning gap in the infrastructure of this great nation. Our country is tied together with a network of cell phone reception towers that is necessary for our quality of life.

According to some study somewhere, American teens spend an average of nine hours a day on their phones, compared to about six hours for those aged eight to twelve. The parents of these unfortunate prodigy, who, if truth be told, would just as soon be on their own phones as talk to another family member, drive the family out into the wilderness where they have to go cold turkey with no devices just because some tall mountains or big trees get in the way of phone reception.

The fact is, there are embarrassing gaps in cell phone reception all over the Olympic Peninsula. It may not seem like a big deal to you, but you're not a guide in the trenches of the tourist industry dealing with people suffering from device deprivation disorder who discover they have been lured to a backwoods dead zone where their devices don't work. This is a problem!

I have personally observed the seven stages of device deprivation disorder in humans in the wilderness. These include confusion, anxiety, panic, hopelessness, fatigue, social isolation, and a sense of inadequacy. At first, people with dead phones are confused. A dead phone can unleash a flood of emotions that makes people think nobody likes them and, in all probability, nobody does. People on devices have a hard time with personal relationships. They've spent so much time on their phones they've forgotten how to interact with other humans who are not on their phones.

People with dead phones have a lot of anxiety because they think they're missing calls that they won't answer anyway. Missing calls engenders a vague belief that everyone else has it better than you do. They do.

Sufferers of device deprivation often panic while assuming something has gone terribly wrong with their world. It has. They might be forced to talk to other people in an effort to establish human contact without phone service. People deprived of their devices will sometimes feel hopeless when forced to stop and consider the bleak desperation of their pointless existence. That can be a hassle you just don't need.

As long as people are on devices, they are just tired and stressed. Once the device stops working, the thin veneer of civility dissolves, leaving the sufferer tired, stressed, and frustrated. Sometimes, people enduring device deprivation are forced to stop and take notice of the natural world that is all around them. This can be extremely frustrating. They could walk through a forest of thousand-year-old trees, go to a beach where the whales spout, or sit by a waterfall and watch the salmon jump, but not if there is no phone reception. No one is going to like these scenic splendors if you can't get them on social media, so what would be the point of going there? There isn't one.

This can lead to an overwhelming sense of inadequacy, fueled by the belief that everyone else is having a better vacation than you are. They probably are. A modern vacation is like a road rally where destinations are checked off a list at a dizzying rate and can all be ruined by a lapse in phone reception. A dead phone can force tourists to rewrite their whole vacation itinerary in order to go someplace the phone will work. Who needs that?

By neglecting to address the scourge of device deprivation disorder and its effects on the tourist industry, we risk losing our share of the tourist market to areas that provide this essential service. Reliable, universal cell phone coverage in every square inch of this Olympic Peninsula is an idea whose time has come. We'll thank ourselves later if we do the right thing now.

May 4, 2022

20

THE BEARS ARE AWAKE

"Where can I see a bear?" the frantic tourist asked. This is a common question among the seasonal visitors to the emerald-green playground we call home. It is not a particularly easy one to answer. Bears seem to be about the number one critter that tourists want to see. Ironically, people are about the last thing bears want to see.

There could be many reasons for this. In my experience in the trenches of the tourist industry, people invariably start screaming, "Bear!" when they see one. This scares the bear and sends it skedaddling before you can even get a good look at it. That's because bears are generally a lot smarter than most other creatures. They don't stand around after they get yelled at. Bears have a lot of emotional baggage left over from hunting season. It's a grudge the bears are not likely to forget.

As the old saying goes, if a pine needle falls in the forest, an eagle sees it, a deer hears it, and a bear smells it. Meanwhile, humans are nearly blind unless the light is right. Our ears have been deafened by technology. We have a crummy sense of smell from living in a polluted environment. Bears have an incredible sense of smell with noses said to be seven times more sensitive than a bloodhound's. They can be stinky too. The scent of a bear is not too unlike that of a horse with a musky tang, unless they have been rolling in an elk carcass, which some suggest might be in an effort to find a mate. This would be another case of don't knock it until you've tried it.

Smelling the near presence of a bear in the woods gives you a feeling like you are never truly alone, but chances are, you probably won't see it. Our bears are shy. Bear attacks are practically unheard of except for a couple of bear hunters who were chewed up. We suspect they had it coming. Right now, the bears are fresh out of hibernation. They're grazing on grass and on the hunt for elk calves, deer fawns, and bird nests, among other things. Bears are omnivores, which means they can eat anything that isn't nailed down.

Scientists tell us that bears do not attain a state of true hibernation like our iconic Olympic marmots or members of Congress. Bears reach a state of torpor that some of us humans might attain while watching golf on TV. Every once in a while, you might wake up for a beer commercial before you doze back off. That is not hibernation.

Bears are extremely intelligent. People like to argue whether bears are smarter than wolves or cougars, and I think they are. Our Olympic timber wolves were bounty hunted into extermination with poison, snares, and traps ninety years ago. The bears are still here; case closed. As for cougars, they are awesome predators, but no one has ever reported them breaking into a vehicle.

Bears, on the other hand, are experts at breaking into anything. The old joke is that they seldom break out through the same hole they broke into. I once found a cabin where a bear broke in through the door and went out through the roof. I watched a small bear about the size of a German Shepherd break into a microbus at the Whiskey Bend trailhead. I tried to say something, but the little bear growled and it wasn't my van. Forget about bears being smarter than wolves or cougars. They may be smarter than people.

May 6, 2024

21

THE GREEN CRAB BLUES

It was another tough week in the news for our environment. The green crab is an invasive species first noticed in Willapa Bay in 1961. By the late 1990s, the green crab was found from California to British Columbia. Lately, they have infested the Strait of Juan de Fuca and have been found in Dungeness Bay. This sent a shock wave through the ranks of the old-time crabbers, who remember the old days when crabbing was all that really mattered. The month of May brought the really big Dungeness crab into the bay to mate and lay their eggs. Dungeness crabs are cannibals. You want a good hard shell when mating with a cannibal. The crab caught in the spring of the year were in prime shape with hard shells and legs full of sweet meat that could be cooked in any number of ways with the clams, oysters, flounder, sturgeon and salmon caught in the bay while crabbing.

Dungeness Bay was a hot spot for halibut. The walls of the old Dungeness Tavern were lined with black-and-white pictures of giant halibut caught right out in front of the tavern in the bay. The old Native American method of getting the big halibut was to dig a gunny sack full of butter clams, smash them with an ax, and throw the sack overboard in a likely spot. When the halibut grabbed the sack and started shaking it around, you hooked up the biggest herring you could find, sent it down to the bottom, and it was fish on!

Those were the good old days, but the good old days were too good to last. These days, nearly every species of fish and shellfish in

Dungeness Bay is either threatened, polluted, or just plain gone. The most abundant species seems to be the hundreds of seals littering the sandbars whose bathroom habits can produce a bacteria bloom with unpronounceable names.

Now we have those pesky, invasive green crabs, which we are told will eat up and despoil everything the seals don't eat or pollute first. Fortunately, state, federal, and tribal co-managers are studying the problem. These myriad government agencies have many years of experience eradicating marine species from our environment with the best available science.

Remember the true cod? They used to be thick. You almost always caught true cod when you went salmon fishing. They were great for fish and chips. We got rid of true cod by dragging nets across the sea floor where the fish fed on candlefish. Candlefish got their name because when dried, they are so oily you can light them and they will burn like fish-scented candles. Many fish eat candlefish, so they burrow in the gravel. Salmon are sometimes caught with gravel in their gills, which they probably picked up snatching candlefish.

Bottom-dragging trawl nets plow the candlefish beds in a two-pronged approach that eliminates the candlefish and the fish that feed on them. Eliminating food sources such as candlefish, smelt, and herring has gone a long way toward reducing salmon, halibut, and bottom fish populations. The once-popular Dungeness Bay Spring Chinook fishery used to run through May and June. You could just row your boat out into Dungeness Bay without a motor and catch king salmon. This fishery has been closed due to a failure of our fisheries co-managers to restore the Spring Chinook. Coincidentally, the production of Dungeness River hatchery salmon and steelhead that allowed for these world-class fisheries has been eliminated, curtailed, or just plain shut down. Admittedly, it took decades of tireless effort in addition to the best available science to achieve these results.

In fact, it has been a real challenge to manage a heretofore-perceived inexhaustible fisheries resource into endangered species, but it was worth it. Millions have been spent building logjams, building bridges, planting native vegetation, and buying property from willing sellers with predictable results. The fish remain endangered.

The co-managers need only apply these same methods to the green crab for an inexhaustible source of grant funding. In 2022, Washington governor Jay Inslee declared war on the green crab, forking over almost nine million dollars to fund a committee of co-managers to study the problem. In 2023, 180,000 green crabs were removed from Willapa Bay and Grays Harbor. Meanwhile, it is illegal for people to catch or possess the green crab. While this may seem counterintuitive to the management of an invasive species that could create an environmental disaster to our marine resources, it all makes sense if you follow the money.

The Washington Department of Fish and Wildlife maintains that Washingtonians are too ignorant to tell the difference between a green crab and native crab. This ignores the fact that we have to identify myriad species to fish or hunt in Washington or risk being fined.

There are eight species of trout in Washington that you must identify in case you catch one. In many waters, you can keep a cutthroat trout but not a rainbow or a bull trout. Don't know the difference? That can get you a ticket. There are five species of salmon you may or may not possess depending on the area, seasons, size, and bag limits. In addition, sometimes you must turn loose a fish with an adipose fin indicating it is an unclipped hatchery fish. Don't know what an adipose fin is? The fish cops will be more than willing to help you with that. There are twelve species of rockfish which the WDFW fishing pamphlet describes as "challenging to identify." Some of them you can keep and some you must release or face fines, but it is up to the angler to figure it out. We have four species of shrimp. Each has different seasons and bag limits. We have eight species of clams. Some clam limits are by weight and others list the number and size of the clams you may keep. Caution is advised.

If you think fishing, shrimping, and clamming is too complicated, then forget about hunting. You're allowed four grouse per day but not more than three dusky, spruce, or ruffed grouse. Confused? Don't go duck hunting. You're allowed seven ducks but only one pintail and only two mallard hens. Can't identify a duck flying forty-five miles an hour? Don't go goose hunting. We have seven subspecies of Canada geese. To hunt some of these subspecies, you must take a test and pass with an 80 percent score or forget about your Christmas goose.

Still, the WDFW is convinced that Washingtonians are too stupid to identify a green crab. We are forced to release them back into the water where they threaten the destruction of our marine environment. Oregonians are a lot more intelligent. They can identify green crabs. In fact, it is illegal in Oregon to release them. Why on Earth would Washington want to protect the green crab? In Maine, they're called "a most delicious scourge." They figure, if you can't beat them, eat them.

That makes too much sense to ever work here where they say don't eat them, we need them for our new grant-funded revenue stream. Having spent the last sixty years studying green crab, bureaucracies are poised to spring into action and manage them for the benefit of government agencies everywhere. With any luck at all, they can keep the green crab populations healthy, ensuring sufficient funding to continue studying the problem for another sixty years. It's the least we can do.

May 8, 2024

22

NO SELFIES IN THE OUTHOUSE

This year's tourist migration seems even heavier than last year's mob scene. While tourists keep the lights on, people can go crazy when they escape the city and enter the woods or the water. I blame the media. City folks watch nature shows telling them animals are just like people and some people are just too pushy for their own good. They get too close, harassing animals that don't like people. The animal shows are punctuated with commercials showing SUVs plunging through streams, beaches, and mountaintops like the world is their race track. All of this fosters the crazy idea that if we spend enough money and do crazy things in the wilderness, someone will like us on social media, even if it kills us.

The smartphone is an amazing gadget that has become the most important component of any modern vacation. It's as if you have to constantly take pictures of yourself on vacation to prove to the world that you actually went somewhere and were having a wonderful time. This same smartphone gets people into a lot of trouble every year. It can be easy to get lost in the woods while relying on a phone for navigation. Many hikers take a smartphone along on their journeys instead of a map and a compass. Then, for whatever reason (the weather, lack of coverage, or dead batteries), the phone is useless, leaving the hiker with no idea where he or she is or how to signal for help.

Taking selfies can be self-destructive behavior, like the guy who fell off the edge of the seventy-five-foot-high Sol Duc Falls while taking a selfie a few years ago. At least someone got a video of it. The Sol Duc Falls is much more than just an iconic National Park destination. Over the years, it's been a tourist magnet, luring them like lemmings to the edge of the cliff, past the warning signs, and over the safety railing, where it does not go well. One guy (why is it generally a guy?) climbed over the railing at the edge of the falls and wound up falling to the bottom, where he was trapped and suffering from hypothermia. Other hikers called 911 and lowered supplies down to him with their shoestrings. An amazing YouTube video shows him climbing out of the falls by sticking a pocket knife in a log and pulling himself up and out of the canyon five minutes before search and rescue teams arrived. We don't know if he got a selfie.

A week later, the Olympic Peninsula made the national news with a big story about a woman who got into a pile of trouble losing her phone up in the outhouse on Walker Mountain. While it is unsure at this time if she was taking a selfie, the Walker Mountain outhouse is among the most scenic sanitary facilities on the Olympic Peninsula. Somehow, the phone was dropped into the outhouse. The owner fell in after it trying to lower herself down with a dog leash to retrieve the phone. She obviously had not purchased phone insurance but gets points for style. Search and rescue came to the rescue. They rescued the woman and recommended she seek medical attention.

Let's review a couple of safety dos and don'ts for tourist season. Do tell someone where you're going and when you'll get back. Do take the ten survival gear essentials on your wilderness trip. Don't take selfies in the outhouse.

May 10, 2022

23

SEARCHING FOR SOLITUDE

Now that the tourists are here, it's easy to see why we put a season on them in the first place. From the acidified ocean to the melting glaciers and the majestic rainforests in between, the Olympic Peninsula has seen an unprecedented invasion of tourists searching for solitude in a pristine wilderness while waiting in line for ferries, burgers, ice cream, and National Park entrances.

Here in Washington, it's illegal to bait waterfowl and bears, but baiting the tourists with tall tales has been a proud Peninsula tradition since the first European arrived on our shores. These early tourists all had one thing in common. No one believed them when they got back home.

The Strait of Juan de Fuca was named after a tourist who may or may not have actually been here. The Greek navigator Apostolos Valerianos, who went by the name of Juan de Fuca, claimed that in 1592, he found an inlet on the Pacific coast in which he sailed for twenty days in a land rich in gold, silver, and pearls. The Spanish, English, Russian, and American tourists spent the next two hundred years looking for this mythical Northwest Passage, an imaginary shortcut across the continent to the treasures of the Orient.

It wasn't until July 1787 that the first documented European tourists, Captain Charles Barkley and his wife, Frances, sailed their ship the *Imperial Eagle* into the Strait of Juan de Fuca. The results were catastrophic for the Native Americans, who regaled the subsequent invasion of European explorers and settlers with stories about how they never went into the Olympic Mountains. The mountains were haunted by a tribe of hairy, giant cannibals and a thunderbird big enough to pluck whales out of the ocean and drop them on the glaciers to save them for later. Recent archaeological discoveries and tribal testimonies have shown that the Olympics were inhabited for thousands of years with camps and trails to villages all through the mountains.

Obviously, the Native Americans wanted to keep the Olympics for themselves. Our pioneer forebears had their own ideas about baiting tourists. They said all you had to do was push a boat up the Elwha River far enough, and you'd find a lake and a prairie and maybe even some Indians who still hunted buffalo. Hearing this tall tale, the Press Expedition of 1898 wasted no time in buying some green lumber from one of the pioneer forefathers to build a boat to find the lake.

The expedition spent weeks building and pushing the leaky boat up the Elwha through the snow, ice, and logjams. Abandoning the boat, they discovered a camp of S'Klallam elk hunters with a big fire and elk quarters hanging.

The S'Klallam claimed they knew nothing about the upper Elwha country, confirming the usual story that no Indian would ever venture up there. However, there is little doubt that by then, the news had traveled through the moccasin telegraph about the white man wiping out the buffalo, and the locals didn't want the same thing to happen to the elk. That would come later.

Throughout the early 1900s, the locals told the tourists this was the last frontier. They bragged of the great mineral wealth that was waiting to be discovered in the Olympics. Mountains, streams, and lakes were named after the gold, silver, iron, copper, and coal you were sure to find if you had enough venture capital. Promotions like these put Tull City on the map.

These days, tourists are lured to the Peninsula searching for solitude on a crowded planet—with thousands of their closest friends. They follow a conga line of traffic jams to wait for hours to get into a National Park entrance gate. They hike with a mob to someplace they saw a picture of on the internet. Then, they complain that they couldn't take a picture of the scenic splendor because there were too many people blocking their view. It's the end of the last frontier.

May 15, 2021

24

THE STORY OF LIGHTNING BOLDT

Lightning Boldt is a biography of Judge George H. Boldt by John C. Hughes, chief historian for the Office of Secretary of State. It's a fascinating read for anyone interested in the history of fishing in Washington. Hughes sat in Boldt's courtroom and witnessed the trial that reaffirmed Native Americans' right to up to 50 percent of the harvestable salmon and established them as co-managers of the fisheries with the state. The decision was upheld by the US Supreme Court.

Judge Boldt was called "Lightning" for his reputation of speed and efficiency in throwing the book at mobsters, tax evaders, and corrupt union leaders. The son of Danish immigrants, Boldt was born in Chicago in 1903. He graduated from high school in Stevensville, Montana. The town was named after Isaac Stevens, a multi-tasker who became Washington's first territorial governor, railroad surveyor, and superintendent of Indian affairs.

In the 1850s, Stevens negotiated ten treaties where the Native Americans agreed to give up 100,000 square miles of their lands so Europeans could homestead it. The treaties routinely guaranteed that "the right of taking fish, at all usual and accustomed grounds and stations, is further secured to said Indians in common with all citizens of the Territory." At the time, salmon runs were considered inexhaustible, so giving the Indians a right they already had was not a problem. During negotiations for the treaty at the Chehalis River, Stevens sweetened the deal with one hundred bushels of potatoes. The treaties were translated from English into dozens of Indian languages through the Chinook Jargon, a three hundred-word pidgin mix of French, English, and Indian words. The ethnologist James Swan called it "a poor medium of conveying intelligence."

It didn't matter, since the treaties were largely ignored until more than one hundred years later when George Boldt presided over the case of *United States v. State of Washington*. It's ironic that the tribes did not want Boldt on the case because he was such an ardent fisherman. They assumed he was racist. They probably didn't know about Boldt's World War II service in Burma as an OSS intelligence officer with a team of Nisei interpreters. These were Japanese Americans serving in the armed forces. While 110,000 Japanese Americans were placed in internment camps during the war, the Nisei servicemen were described by Boldt as "creditable American citizens given the toughest, dirtiest and most hazardous jobs in the war. Their record is equaled by few and excelled by none." Boldt's detachment rescued three hundred airmen who had crashed behind enemy lines.

After the war, Boldt stated America was a land where racism had no place. Boldt called himself a "4th of July Man," alluding to his love of country, the law, his faith, and his family. He was called a "senile old Indian lover" by white fishermen who burned his effigy. It was said he was married to an Indian. His wife was Scottish. The violent reaction to his decision shocked Boldt, who responded by saying the case should have been brought fifty years prior.

The Boldt decision set off what was known as the Fish War, where each side of the dispute tried to kill the last fish. Fifty years later, many of our salmon runs are endangered or extinct. Fifty years from now, if we continue to ignore our responsibility to restore our fisheries, we'll have only paper fish. The tribes regained their fishing rights, but with that came the responsibility to do something the state can't or won't do: restore our fisheries. If the tribes fail in their responsibility, they'll find half of nothing is nothing and the Boldt decision might just as well have given them half of the buffalo.

May 15, 2024

25

THE FATE OF THE FISH DUCKS

For some, the new year begins on January 1. Out on our rivers, the new year begins with the emergence of the baby salmon from the gravel they were planted in the previous fall. This is a cause for celebration. After a century of overfishing, pollution, environmental destruction, and government policies that doom them to extinction, it's not a question of what happened to the salmon, but why there is one salmon left. The fact that the salmon have survived volcanoes, ice ages, and the invention of nylon testifies to just how hard it's been to eliminate this most important element in our ecosystem, the salmon.

Most everyone is familiar with the water cycle: water evaporates from the ocean to form clouds that travel inland to drop water, forming rivers that flow back into the ocean. The salmon cycle operates in the same way, exchanging energy from the ocean to the mountains and back, sustaining all life along the river, from the smallest bug to the largest tree with the spawned-out remains of their bodies. That cycle is just beginning now. Little schools of these tiny fish are wiggling out of the rocks to swim down the rivers on their years-long journey to the ocean and back. It is a hazardous journey where everything wants to eat them.

Let's start with the mergansers. The male merganser, with his green head and large white belly, looks like a drake mallard. Instead of having a duck bill like a mallard, the merganser has a pointed, serrated beak it uses to catch fish. Its feet are located toward the rear of the bird for maximum underwater propulsion. Even the white belly is a form of camouflage that makes the bird difficult for the fish to see from below.

In comparison, female mergansers have a boring camouflage of brown, black, and gray with a pathetic little red crest on top. She's built to blend in. She'll be making her nest in a hollow of a cottonwood tree while the male migrates to Alaska with his pals to take care of his feathers.

Once the chicks hatch, they have to jump out of the nest and hit the ground running for the river that's high from melting snow. This is a well-disciplined brood that sometimes rides down the rapids on their mother's back. The chicks grow up fast on a diet of regurgitated fish. Eventually, the mother will teach her chicks to hunt fish by swimming along with their heads under water looking for prey, a practice that some uncharitable bird-watchers compare to texting while driving.

I once saw a mother merganser with twenty-one chicks. While the numbers of baby mergansers hatched by their mothers in a given year may not be an indication of the health of a salmon population on a salmon river, it will have to do until a better method comes along.

Twenty years ago, it was not uncommon to see a mother fish duck with a dozen or more chicks. This year, merganser broods are averaging about four or five. With the salmon gone, the animals and birds that depended on them are going away too. The forest itself is malnourished without the fertilization the spawned-out salmon carcasses provide.

Then, there is the human cost of the extinction of the salmon. Much like the elimination of the mergansers, the extinction of the salmon has largely eliminated the culture of fishing among the people who depended on salmon for their food and livelihood. With the salmon gone, people who fish for them could share the unfortunate fate of the fish ducks.

June 1, 2021

26

THE WOODPECKER WARS

All I wanted was a quiet place at the end of the road in the rainforest where I could write my memoirs. It took me years to become an overnight excess with a publishing empire stretching from Oil City to Whiskey Flats, dedicated to shining the light of freedom, truth, and justice as the only wilderness gossip columnist in America, whatever that meant. If I could just find the time. Something was always interrupting. It's all part of the nightmare we call country living.

It started with the drumming. It was sort of a Bo Diddley-on-a-bender beat that just kept going and going and wouldn't stop. Naturally, I assumed it was just another Sasquatch drum circle heating up. Sometimes, I think that's all they do. Maybe I should apologize, but somebody has to work. Financing the hunt for Bigfoot and baiting them takes major funding. Peanut butter and jam sandwiches don't grow on trees.

I opened the door and stuck my head out, ready to holler into the woods to get them to pipe down for a while, and then I saw the real reason for my disturbance. A woodpecker with a bright red head and a great big beak was drilling a hole in the side of the house. Woodpeckers are some of the dumbest creatures on the planet. Maybe it's because they spend their lives beating their heads against trees. It only makes sense that an ecological niche that involves brain damage could lead to an evolutionary dead end.

Shooting the woodpecker was not an option. That would

61

contravene the Geneva Convention of Bird-Watching and possibly upset the neighbors. There are simple rules to get along in the country, like drive slowly, mind your own business, and don't spray the neighbors with birdshot. They could shoot back. Besides, you have a lot better chance of borrowing stuff from the neighbors if you don't shoot at them first.

Not to mention woodpeckers are a protected species. The birds seem to sense this. When I tried to scare it away, the woodpecker looked at me like I was impacting his habitat. I thought we could all just get along, but this is a curse I would not wish on my best enemy. First, there is the endless process of building the nest, which means they have to pull the pink fiberglass insulation out of the wall, scatter it over the yard, and replace it with a flammable nest made of moss and dry twigs. Eventually, the baby birds hatch. You will know this from their constant shrieking for food from dawn till dark for weeks on end. There's a distinctive aroma wafting through the wall, indicating a congealing mass of rotting bird nests just waiting to be used again next year.

Something had to be done. I waited until the woodpecker entered the cavern it had dug in the side of my house and sprang into action. It was going to be too easy. I grabbed a fish net and beat on the wall. When the woodpecker flew out of the hole, I caught it in a fish net and drove into town to turn it loose. I could not imagine a crueler fate. That was until I returned home to find another woodpecker had beat me back to the hole.

The net trick wouldn't work anymore. I had to borrow a ladder from the neighbor and nail a board over the woodpecker hole. For a moment, there was peace. I'd just sat down to type a really good column for once. Then, I heard a woodpecker beating another hole in the wall. Here we go again.

June 5, 2019

27

STRAWBERRY FIELDS

Summer makes me think of my childhood on the Olympic Peninsula. It was the late Pleistocene. The glaciers of the continental ice sheet had melted away to reveal a rich pasturage for vast herds of mammoths, mastodons, and buffaloes, whose bones litter the landscape to this day. Anthropologists have long speculated that the extinction of these Pleistocene megafauna occurred shortly after the arrival of early humans. As a boy, I imagined the thrill of chucking a bone-tipped spear at a big, hairy elephant. Archaeological remains suggest the animals were ambushed at the water holes. Perhaps they were driven by fire. It must have been like fish in a barrel! As a kid, I figured it was just my bum luck that all the good hunting was done by the time I got here. By then, the lowlands were filled in with farms. Children were considered farm machinery. There were many fine farm careers to choose from. I couldn't wait to get started.

Picking strawberries seemed like easy money. We started out early on a summer morning, gorging down an endless row of perfectly ripe berries. That was strawberry heaven, until your gut hurt so bad you could not walk upright, which started the endless trips to the outhouse where you spotted a fellow sucker-puncher from school. This started the berry fight. That's where you had to be careful. You could be fired for berry fights. Once you were fired, there was no more dough for the things you really need for a happy childhood, like fireworks and fishing gear. This was the bad old days before enlightened parents gave their kids debit cards to manage their money. So, you didn't want to get caught throwing berries even at somebody who was asking for it by throwing berries at you. No. Revenge could wait. There would be many trips to the outhouse those first couple of days of berry picking until you were so sick of eating berries you'd just as soon chew on a clump of kale.

As luck would have it, the boss kept all the boys picking together where he could keep an eye on them. No matter what, the other guy's row of berries always seemed to be a little riper with a few more of the really big strawberries that could fill up your boxes faster. It was against the rules to pick on another picker's row, but nobody said anything about swapping boxes with them. Just for fun, I liked to exchange a specially prepared "sucker-box" with my friend. That was a box of rocks covered with a thin layer of camouflage berries. It was a dirty trick, but my friend had it coming. We both did, as it turned out.

As the day in the berry field wore on, your back began to ache from the constant strain of bending. Your knees were shot from crawling down the endless rows. You were only paid for the berries you picked and if you ate all the berries you picked, you paid in many ways, including gastric distress that kept you dashing for the outhouse. That was the bad news. The good news was it was probably the only shade in the field.

After what seemed like all day, it was quitting time. The pickers lined up for their pay but I didn't get mine. It seemed I had a box of rocks in my berries. I'd been sucker-boxed!

I went on to pick many other crops after that: berries, beans, and peas. These days, it seems like farms are rare mastodons. It makes you wonder where we'll get our food.

June 27, 2007

28

THE *CADBORO* INCIDENT

July 4, 1828 was a day that would live in infamy, if anyone remembered. That's when the Hudson Bay schooner *Cadboro* destroyed an S'Klallam village in Dungeness Bay with cannon fire. It was part of what Chief Factor John McLoughlin called a "punitive expedition" against the S'Klallam for the killing of HBC trader Alexander McKenzie and four company employees on Hood Canal. It seems McKenzie, who had just walked from Fort Vancouver, had hired two S'Klallam youths to paddle their canoe from Port Gamble to Port Angeles, across the Strait of Juan de Fuca to Victoria, then on to Langley, British Columbia before returning to Port Gamble. The fact this voyage would be completed in an open dugout canoe in the dead of winter with no more preparation than we might make on a simple business trip proves that the old-timers around here were of a different breed.

Trader McKenzie was a mean one. He beat and kicked the lads who were paddling the canoes and then refused to pay the boy's father for their services. That was a not a good idea. The S'Klallam had a reputation for being warlike since July of 1788, when the Englishman Robert Duffin piloted a longboat down the Strait of Juan de Fuca, where it was "pierced by a thousand arrows." McKenzie should have known better. He camped without placing a guard. He and his party of four were killed that night on a place called Deadman's Spit ever since. A woman traveling with the party was taken captive.

When word got back to Fort Vancouver, Chief Factor John McLoughlin, a man known for his violent outbursts of temper, decided to send a military force to Puget Sound as a warning to all the tribes that HBC fur brigades and traders were not to be harassed. On June 17, trader Alexander McLeod left Fort Vancouver with a force of sixty-three men bound for Puget Sound. There, they were to meet the *Cadboro,* which had sailed from the Columbia River to meet them. Included in the party were two Iroquois and two "Owhyees," or Hawaiians.

The Iroquois had worked for the HBC as voyagers and mercenaries. They had a reputation as fierce warriors, no less than the Hawaiians, so they must have got along well. A clerk with the expeditions describes how the "Iroquois, Owyhees, and Chinooks [a tribe from southwest Washington] painted themselves ready for battle." It was not much of a battle. The S'Klallam had reportedly prepared for the assault by wetting their blankets to ward off cannon balls, which would illustrate the level of cultural misunderstanding.

On the morning of July 4, while negotiations were still underway for the release of the captive, who the clerk referred to as "this Helen of ours who will cause a siege as long as that of Troy," the *Cadboro* opened fire with three cannons, destroying the village and forty-six canoes. The captive woman and some of McKenzie's effects were recovered.

The expedition returned to Vancouver having killed twenty-seven people, including women and children, and burning another village in Port Townsend on the way. Trader McLeod was said to be pleased, but the destruction of property was judged to be injurious to business. MacLeod was not promoted to Chief Factor by the HBC. Those who ignore history are doomed to watch television.

July 1, 2015

29

THERE WALKS A LOGGER

That great American philosopher Buzz Martin, also known as "The Singing Logger," said, "There walks a logger there walks a man." I can think of no greater tribute to my old friend Jim Anderson. He logged and built roads in the high country that was as steep as the back side of God's head. This was back when they cut old-growth timber, not the toothpicks they harvest today.

No, these were real logs. Jim told me about a spruce that was so big it wouldn't fit on a log truck. They had to buck the log into short sections and stand them on end on a low-boy trailer. That must have been a thrill to meet on the narrow, winding road around Lake Crescent.

There were plenty of thrills logging in those days. Just getting to work was half the job. It was a two-hour-plus drive part way in the dark to the upper drainages of the west end of the Olympic Peninsula. Once he got to the job, the real work started: packing dynamite and setting chokers behind a Cat. That was a D9 Caterpillar, a steel monstrosity that carved roads up the mountains.

It was a scene of many near-death experiences for Jim. One time, the D9 Cat came rolling down the mountain straight at him when he was stuck in a hole in the downed timber. He said you really do see your life flash before your eyes before you die. Luckily, the Cat stopped, which gave Jim the opportunity for many more near-death experiences before he quit the woods and went to work in a pulp mill.

But the pulp mill was not his true calling. Jim was a hunter-gatherer in the tradition of our ancestors, when we relied on natural foods for our survival. Where there was edible wild food to be had, Jim caught it, shot it, or picked it. Hunting with Jim could be an embarrassment. One time, he shot a running deer that I had missed when it was standing still. Fishing with Jim on the Lyre River could be humiliating.

Jim would most likely already have a fish on the beach by the time I got to the fishing hole. Sometimes, he caught both our limits before I got my gear put together. It was like he only took me along to help pack the fish. That was okay; I'd pack his fish any day, except for the day he caught seventeen steelhead in Salt Creek. That would have been a problem, but he only kept two.

Jim was a witness to the destruction of the fisheries of the Olympic Peninsula. He went to Peninsula College, attending the now discontinued fisheries program. It gave him a scientific perspective on the extinction of our salmon and how they could be restored. More than that, Jim was a keen natural observer and a gifted writer.

Jim wrote his own obituary. In it, he described our favorite fishing hole, Freshwater Bay. He said,

> The sun is just beginning to peek above the water and the first rays of sunlight shine off the cliffs, birds and salmon are feeding on baitfish on the edge of the kelp beds. It is one of those days where you hook a King Salmon with each pass and you don't want to stop. Just one more pass before you are called home.

He's home now. It's like Buzz Martin said: "If you get to heaven, you'll find more than one set of cork boot tracks on those streets of gold. There walks a logger. There walks a man."

July 8, 2020

30

PIRATES, PATRIOTS, AND PLUNDERERS

A lady sailed into Port Angeles last week. She seemed out of time and out of place with an aura of history when the New World was ripe for the taking. Her beauty was unmistakable. Her past was unforgivable, but she was a lady just the same.

Named after Martha Washington, the *Lady Washington* set out from Boston in 1787 under Captain Robert Gray, who had served as a privateer during the Revolutionary War. She carried a cargo of trade goods for the fur trade on the northwest coast on a voyage that made her the first American ship to round Cape Horn. She was the first American vessel to land on the west coast of North America when she made landfall at Tillamook Bay in Oregon in1788. In 1789, she entered the Strait of Juan de Fuca. Her crew traded sea otter skins at Neah Bay until rough seas drove her north where she was the first ship to circumnavigate Vancouver Island. Later, she became the first American vessel to reach Japan, Hawaii, and Hong Kong.

It's hard to imagine the dangers she faced while approaching uncharted coastlines protected by reefs and fog and armored with treacherous rocks while her crew attempted to trade with the native inhabitants who were known to capture ships and slaughter the crews—with good reason.

Robert Gray, who later discovered the Columbia River, legitimizing America's claim to the west coast of North America, was captain of the *Lady Washington* on a voyage to the Queen Charlotte Islands (now Haida Gwaii). He ordered his crew to burn a village said to be a half a mile across that contained an estimated two hundred houses.

Known for a reckless bravery, a mercurial temper, and attention to business detail, Captain Gray was a successful trader who defied the monopoly of the British East India Trading Company by taking his furs to China to trade for tea, silk, porcelain, and fabrics he would sail back to Boston.

Gray's partner in crime, Captain John Kendrick, was known to be intemperate and unstable with a reputation his financiers claimed was "suspended between the qualifications of egregious knavery and incredible stupidity."

Captain Kendrick was not known to be a good trader. He sailed the *Lady Washington* to Japan, where he was unable to sell any furs. He then ended up in the Philippines, where the *Lady Washington* was wrecked. *Lady Washington*'s captains, Gray and Kendrick, were either pirates, patriots, or plunderers, depending on which side of this global trade you were on.

In 1989, as part of Washington's centennial, the *Lady Washington* was rebuilt. Since then, she has sailed the Pacific coast as a living maritime museum. This is still hazardous. The *Lady Washington* ran aground in 2013 in Grays Harbor and at the mouth of Sequim Bay in 2017. This was nothing compared to the original *Lady Washington*'s battering somewhere in southeast Alaska in the spring of 1788. There, she was hurled up onto the rocks then hauled off minus her jib and bowsprit. She was still watertight though badly in need of repairs.

Nowadays, people get upset if highway construction delays them a few minutes or if the Hood Canal Bridge inconveniences them by making them wait for a ship to get through. Imagine a day when you could not go anywhere until the wind and tides were favorable.

You waited on anchor or sailed in circles while the worms ate holes in your wooden hull and the crew died of scurvy. Things have changed, but still *Lady Washington* dropped by Port Angeles to wait for a weather window for a safe return to her home port of Aberdeen. We wished the lady godspeed.

July 10, 2019

31

STUPID CAMPING TIPS

It was another tough week in the news. We almost didn't need a bombshell press release from Olympic National Park to ruin our weekend with yet another example of how Mother Nature is revolting. The Olympics don't have any dangerous animals like grizzlies or rattlers, but tourists get into trouble anyway.

It seems that a number of the "beautiful and iconic" Roosevelt elk that inhabit the Hoh Rainforest are showing signs of becoming "habituated or abnormally comfortable with the presence of humans. People have been approaching the elk too closely, risking serious injury. This creates a dangerous situation for both the visitors and the elk." It is a crisis that has prompted park officials to recommend a safe distance of at least one hundred feet when viewing elk and other wildlife. We put that in the "duh" file. It's yet another example of senseless government warnings like the labels that tell us not to stick our head in a bucket or put fish hooks in our mouths. Does the government really think we are that stupid? Yes, only because we are.

The Roosevelt elk is a sensitive, intelligent woodland creature. A bull elk can be an extremely unpredictable thousand-pound animal with a mess of ivory tipped spikes on his head. Moving closer than one hundred feet away from an elk is not a good idea unless it is elk hunting season. Then it is almost impossible to get within a thousand yards of them. Elk may be just dumb animals, but they are often a

72

lot smarter than humans. The elk are quite aware that there is no elk hunting season in the park, so you would be wise to keep your distance.

Here are some other stupid camping tips:

1. Stay away from the skunks. Skunks are sensitive, intelligent woodland creatures, but they can be very territorial and you never know if you're camping in their territory.
2. Don't use gasoline to start your campfire. We've all seen it done, but gasoline is more explosive than dynamite.
3. Don't start your campfire with dynamite either, and remember, try to keep your campfire under one acre.
4. Don't drink the water. One summer, I ran float trips where we saw a majestic Roosevelt elk lying in the river every day. It was dead. Our waters are polluted with unpronounceable bacteria even when there isn't a dead elk soaking in them.
5. Don't risk eating clams from uncertified sources, but if you do, feed them to your mother-in-law or other loved one first and keep an eye on the person for paralytic shellfish poisoning.

While you're at the beach, never forget these things:

6. Don't sunbathe on barnacles.
7. Don't play on beach logs on an incoming tide. You could be crushed when the waves come in and toss the logs around like bowling pins;
8. Don't go swimming in a riptide.
9. Don't bait the park rangers. They are sensitive, intelligent woodland creatures.
10. Don't ask the park rangers what the elevation at the beach is.

While visiting areas outside of Olympic National Park, be advised:

11. Do not set up your tent in the middle of a logging road.

If you should encounter loggers, remember:

12. They are also sensitive, intelligent woodland creatures—with dynamite.
13. It is wrong to bait the loggers.
14. Do not ask if they are the loggers on TV.
15. Don't ask if you can borrow the logger's chainsaw.
16. Don't ask if they've seen any spotted owls lately.

It is sincerely hoped that by observing these and other stupid camping tips, the tourists will survive long enough to go home.

July 28, 2010

32

ROOT HOG OR DIE

"Root hog or die." If I had a dollar for every-time I heard my Aunt Stella say that, I would never have picked berries for money. It's a phrase that originated with the first colonists in America who turned the hogs loose to forage for themselves.

This led to conflicts with the Native American gardens that were not fenced. Indigenous gardeners grew what they called the three sisters. Corn supported the beans over a ground cover of pumpkins that kept the weeds down. It was a smorgasbord the hogs made short work of. The practice of introducing feral hogs to the environment leapfrogged its way across the country to the Oregon Territory, where the Neals settled in the 1840s.

There, the hogs made short work of the camas, a staple crop that was the main source of carbohydrates since time immemorial in this vast territory where "root hog or die" was a way of life. My Aunt Stella employed this phrase to motivate her crew of kids to get through breakfast and pile into the station wagon for a trip to the berry fields.

These days, it is considered cruel and unusual punishment to make children get up early in the morning and go to work, but that's the way it was back then. Stella would have been up for hours by the time the kids were ready to eat. She had cooked breakfast and made lunch for Uncle Len, who was off to the woods to cut timber. Then, she had her quiet time until she woke up the kids. Stella baked countless loaves of perfect bread, canned everything that grew in her tremendous garden, and made everything else from butter to beer the old-fashioned way with food grown, raised, caught, or shot right there on the farm.

"Root hog or die," she'd say, putting out a spread of eggs, venison sausage, toast, jam, and fruit she'd canned herself. Then, we piled into the station wagon for a dusty ride to the fields where there was money to be made picking berries and beans.

In those days, there was no minimum wage for kids. Your pay was determined by how much you picked. You could make as little or as much as you wanted. As kids, we wanted to make as much money as we possibly could for vital supplies of fireworks and fishing gear. There was only one way to do that.

"Root hog or die."

After about an hour of picking anything, a kid's knees get sore. It gets awfully hot and lunchtime seems about a million hours away. When it does finally come, you are about hungry enough to eat a dirt clod. You wolf down a sandwich made with the most heavenly bread that Aunt Stella might have baked that morning, filled with some kind of lunch meat shot or raised in the back field.

Eventually, after what seemed like a million years, it was time to go home. That meant a long ride down a dirt road with the windows closed to try to keep the dust out. The heat, the dust, and the exhaustion of the day was instantly relieved with a trip to the swimming hole.

Stella didn't swim. She did not have time. If she wasn't cooking, canning, or cleaning she was volunteering at the church, at the school, or in the community. She lived a life of self-reliance and service to others. We miss her now that she's gone, but it's enough to know that somewhere in heaven, there's a root cellar with gleaming rows of her canned preserves where you don't have to root hog or die anymore.

July 31, 2019

33

MENTAL WELLNESS DAYS

There are no mental wellness days here at Hoh River Rafters, because you'd have to be crazy to work here. We are in the trenches in the tourist industry. Tourism is a pipeline for a forced migration of desperate travelers seeking someplace cool in our heat-stricken nation. These are the climate refugees whose hometowns are being deep fried with an unseasonably warm triple-digit heat wave that has them fleeing thousands of miles north.

There are so many Texans here now it makes you wonder if there is anybody left in Texas. Arizona, Nevada, Utah, and California must be deserted for the same reason. People want out of those ovens, if only to come here to complain about the weather.

"When will the weather get better?" the tourists ask.

To this, we, as ambassadors of the tourist industry, must reply that most of the time, it is a lot worse. This is in keeping with the goals and objectives of the tourism industry: getting the tourists to go home.

Another goal and objective of the tourist industry is to keep the tourists from killing themselves by doing stupid stuff. Perhaps it is a symptom of the dumbing down of this great nation or a byproduct of social media that has people risking their lives so the internet will like them.

A young man asked my advice about paddling his pack raft (an inflatable craft, that is, ironically about the size of a coffin) through fifteen miles of open ocean from the mouth of the Hoh River to La Push. I advised him (it's always a guy coming up with these ideas) to check on that life insurance policy.

They all seem to become defensive at this point. All that is left is to plead with these would-be adventurers to not make people come and look for them.

The fact is, we really and truly care about the health, happiness, and welfare of our tourists. If they kill themselves doing stupid stuff, it jacks up our outfitter insurance rates. That is why we have a waiver form where prospective rafters declare that they are physically fit to engage in the activity. It is usually after signing this document that the prospective rafters share the intimate details of their medical histories.

We're not sure why people who've just had back surgery, are recovering from a major heart attack, or recently escaped from a mental institution for the criminally insane would think river rafting is a good idea, and we don't care. We sell raft trips. If we only floated healthy, happy, well-adjusted people down the river, we would seldom be employed. We are dealing with tourists, after all. Our sympathies go with the children, our brightest and best hope for the future. They would rather be playing video games in the basement with a microwave chimichanga and an energy drink. Instead, they are forced into river rafting with either the "lawnmower parent," who enables and smooths the child's path through life, or the "helicopter parent," who asks the child if he or she is okay every fifteen seconds, or both.

Today's children are like hothouse flowers. One mother insisted her daughter was allergic to water, so she gave the child Benadryl as a precaution should the child be accidentally splashed on a raft trip. The other child was hyperactive, so he was on a different medication. While the little girl nodded out, the little boy was bouncing around, screaming and making animal noises. Mom was obviously zonked and nodding out on something else, so I kept the Narcan handy. Dad just wanted a cold beer in the shade. It's all about quality time with the family.

August 1, 2022

34

THE PROBLEM WITH COUGARS

It was another tough week in the news. An eight-year-old boy was attacked by a cougar at Lake Angeles, a popular hiking and camping destination in the mountains above Port Angeles. While cougar attacks are rare, what makes this story even more astonishing is the fact that an eight-year-old hiked up to Lake Angeles in the first place. Walking up to Lake Angeles is not something most grown-ups would attempt, even if they weren't packing their camp on their backs. The kid had to be tough to do it. That could be why he survived. Even more incredible was the story of how the boy's mother ran the cougar off by yelling and screaming at it as her child was being attacked. Fortunately, the boy survived with minor injuries. This is surprising since cougars are capable of taking down two hundred-pound deer and thousand-pound elk. Maybe we don't taste that good to cougars, or perhaps these other large prey animals don't have a fierce mother to protect them.

All of this begs the question: Are cougars dangerous? Duh. In 1917, *The Sequim Press* reported an epic cougar attack in the hills above Sequim. Maggie Schmith and Clifford Heath were driving a team of horses pulling a wagon when a cougar jumped on the horses. Miss Schmith grabbed an ax and drove the cougar off. Mr. Heath whacked the cougar several times with a crosscut saw. The cougar kept jumping at them. The couple slowly backed away a half-mile to a house. Some hound hunters were called and they killed the cougar that was eight foot six inches from its nose to the tip of its tail. The cougar was blind and starving but still attacked a team of horses, a wagon, and a pair of pioneers with an ax and a saw.

Cougars can be dangerous, but compared to what? Cougar attacks are rare, isolated incidents compared to the carnage on our highways in the last couple of weeks. People drove head-on into oncoming vehicles, drove into a building, drove off the road, and flipped over for no apparent reason.

Ask yourself these questions. Has a cougar ever chugged a case of beer and run you off the road? Has a cougar ever passed you around a blind corner? Has a cougar ever slammed on its brakes right in front of you and stopped in the middle of the road just because it felt like it? No. All of this begs the question: What is the most dangerous animal on the Olympic Peninsula: the cougar or the road hog?

Seeing a cougar in the woods is a thrill most people will never experience. There are many old-timers who've lived on the Olympic Peninsula their entire lives and have never seen a cougar. Most of the cougars I've seen were crossing the road like a bolt of brown lightning. They jump out of the ditch, bound off the centerline, and disappear so quickly all you see is a brown streak that moves so fast the brain cannot register what the eyes have seen. Except for the long brown tail that lays out behind the cat like a rudder for balance, that lets you know you've seen a cougar.

The problem with cougars is they invariably attack the wrong people. Instead of attacking a brave boy and his courageous mother, cougars should go after people who deserve it. You know the ones. They leave sacks of garbage and burning campfires in the tinder-dry woods. In a perfect world, these people would be attacked by cougars but they never seem to be.

August 2, 2023

35

TOURISTS' REVENGE

This must be one of the busiest tourist seasons ever. It has the locals hoping that school would hurry up and start so everyone would go back where they came from. Some schools have already started, but that has not slowed the tourist invasion. That's because the beginning of school can cause a whole new wave of tourists to hatch out of somewhere and hit the road. Those are the people who waited for school to start so they could go on vacation without being stuck somewhere with a bunch of kids. In a continuing effort to provide accurate information to the tourist hordes, allow me to take this opportunity to share some real questions asked by real tourists about the Olympic Peninsula in this past summer.

As a fishing and rafting guide, I've had the opportunity to act as an ambassador to the tourist industry by providing helpful, accurate information to visitors to our area in a manner that helps them enjoy this recreational wonderland. Here are a few real tourist questions.

"How long does it take for a deer to turn into an elk?" This may seem ridiculous, but to be fair, it should be noted that many of the tourists asking this question are suffering the combined effects of jet lag, dehydration, sleep deprivation, mixed medications, self-medication, and a diet of chips, gas station sushi, and energy drinks.

Try it sometime. In all probability, it will eventually have you asking how long it takes for the marmots to turn into bears. While there could be a smidgen of alternative evolutionary theories in these inquiries, please remember to be gentle with our tourists. Consider that, but for the grace of God, we might all be tourists someday.

"Does the Hoh River come from Alaska?" Yes. The Hoh River flows underground thousands of miles from the Arctic Circle to bubble out of the Earth's crust way up on Mount Olympus. Efforts to trace the actual path the river takes from Alaska to the Olympic Peninsula have been unsuccessful due to a lack of funding and the resistance by modern science to the theory that the Earth is actually hollow.

"Why is the water blue?" This is a common question that tourists often ask about Lake Crescent and the Hoh River. It should be answered with the knowledge gained from the best available science, which can be pretty boring. There's no reason we can't have a little fun with tourists to make their vacations more memorable. In the state of Washington, it's against the law to bait bears, but there's no law against baiting tourists. Let your conscience be your guide. I like to tell the tourists that the color of the water is determined by what type of dye the park rangers dump in the water each morning when they get to work. Water by itself can be clear and boring. Dyeing the lakes and rivers makes them more colorful and scenic. It's a real aid to the photographer trying to shoot a dramatic nature scene that captures the ephemeral beauty of the lakes and rivers amid the surrounding forest of majestic trees.

"Is there any gold to be found in the Olympics?" With the increasing price of this precious metal, inquiries on where to find it are becoming more frequent. I tell the tourists that, of course, there's tons of gold here. The government just doesn't want you to find it. Good thing I've got a secret map to a number of lost gold mines for five dollars.

While it's fun to have fun with tourists for asking, "Is the weather always like this?" or "Why do loggers wear suspenders?" it should be noted that the tourists are generally a lot smarter than me. After all, many of these tourists have traveled the world while I've been stuck here my whole life, going nowhere fast.

In this age of information, the people who choose to spend their vacations on the Olympic Peninsula really do their research. Our visitors are very much aware of local environmental issues that have made the national news, such as the plight of our southern resident orca and the extinction of our salmon. Every once in a while, a tourist asks a question that's painful to answer. It was the ultimate tourist's revenge when one of them asked, "How has the river changed?"

That hurt. The river has died. Watching the river die was like watching the death of a friend while being told the doctors were doing everything possible to get the person the best medical treatment. It was a death that took forty years to achieve. Back then, the glaciers that fed the river were much larger, and when the spring melt began, the river ran higher, colder, and with more volume longer into the summer.

Along about the middle of August, the spring chinook, which entered the river in the spring and spent the summer in the river ripening their spawn, were laying their eggs in the gravel and carpeting the shore with their dead, spawned-out bodies. The elimination of the spawned-out salmon has changed the river.

Bears came down to the river to catch salmon and spread fish remains across the forest floor. Bears were seen by the Native Americans as the mother of all creatures because they caught more fish than they could eat. They fed the other creatures that couldn't catch fish for themselves. Science has confirmed this relationship by identifying an estimated 137 species of birds and animals that feed on spawned-out salmon. In the process, the remains of the spawned-out salmon were spread across the forest floor, fertilizing the trees. The smell along the river was terrific. The water was alive with salmon thrashing in the shallows, making a commotion that sounded like a herd of elk crossing the creek.

As summer turned into fall, the biggest runs of salmon came upstream. The fall rains would flood the river and tributaries, allowing the salmon access to the tiniest little creeks deep into the forest. They recycled the nutrients from the ocean to the forest and back again in an ecosystem that had functioned since the last ice age—until now.

These days, the air along the river is fresh and pure. That would normally be a good thing, but it is the smell of death on a salmon stream. In the past, people were allowed to help the salmon. They reintroduced fish to streams with no salmon by placing boxes of fertilized salmon eggs in the creeks. The fish would hatch and migrate out to sea without having to be fed at a hatchery for a year. Unfortunately, the use of remote hatch boxes to bring back the salmon in our streams is no longer allowed by the powers that be.

Instead, they build logjams with steel and concrete. They spray herbicides along the river to bring the salmon back. They block salmon streams to count juvenile salmon and call it research. None of these activities have brought the salmon back. Our fisheries have been managed to extinction with the best available science. That's how the river has changed. The truth hurts. I can't make fun of tourist questions anymore.

August 17, 2022

36

THE LAW OF THE SEA

And so, another rafting season passes astern. The glaciers in the high Olympics are shrinking at an increasing rate, which is reflected in the low water. The river is the boss. When the old man river says quit, we do.

This causes reflections on the past season and the people we met. One thing you can say for sure is that kids these days are tough. It is not unusual to see a five-year-old pick up a paddle, pull downriver ten miles, and ask for more, or dive right into another feat of human endurance: swimming in the Hoh River. A lot of Peninsula pioneers never learned to swim because the water was too cold. The nearest some of my old friends got to swimming was the Saturday night bath in a horse trough.

Inevitably, some of the glacial swimmers suffered the effects of hypothermia, which was treated by burying them in hot sand. It seemed to work. Mostly, it was a pretty nice bunch of kids this year. There were, however, exceptions to the rule.

She was what some would call "an old soul" or what others might call a spoiled brat. In other words, the kid was seven years old with an eighty-year-old attitude stuffed inside. She stepped into the raft like she was boarding a yacht, asking, "Do we have to do this?"

To this, I replied, "What a coincidence. I'm asking myself the same question."

"I've been riding in the car for so long it feels like a coffin," she said.

"Do you know what a coffin is?" her father asked. She admitted she didn't. "It's where they put dead people," Dad informed her.

"I feel like I've been in a coffin," she confirmed. Her name was Tallulah, or should have been. Her interests were shopping and fine dining. Travel was not on the list. It seemed like, at the age of seven, she was a jet-setter hopping from New Zealand to Costa Rica, Disneyland, and Disney World before gracing us with her presence on the Hoh River.

"She's not my mom," Tallulah said, pointing to the woman sitting with her dad. She continued to delineate the intricacies of the modern blended family as the parental units sitting in the front of the raft visibly squirmed.

One thing was for sure: Tallulah was not going swimming. In fact, just getting wet was out of the question due to her wardrobe issues. She was wearing a silk blouse and had no intention of getting it wet, wrinkled, or both.

Just then, disaster struck. The inevitable splash came and errant drops of water came in contact with the silk, causing an outburst from Tallulah.

"Calm down," a parental unit pleaded, with predictable results.

"You're not my mom!" Tallulah replied.

"I can have it dry cleaned and back to you by morning," I lied. The best I could do for laundry was to stick it in a bucket and swish it around with a plunger, but by then we had a different problem.

"My tooth is loose," Tallulah informed us. Then, her tooth just fell out, causing a sense of panic for all aboard. It was my duty to inform the party that, due to the maritime law of the sea and the powers vested in me as captain of the vessel, I was entitled to a share of the Tooth Fairy money. The crew greeted the news with silence. Tallulah said she'd never heard of such a thing. I told her it was in the waiver form. And just like that, getting wet was not such a big deal any more.

August 31, 2022

37

THE MIRACLE OF THE SALMON

This year's big run of humpies, or pink salmon, in the Dungeness River is like a miracle. It brings to mind the first recorded "Miracle of the Salmon," which happened at a Shaker meeting at Jamestown in 1921.

The Shakers are a Native American branch of Christianity that began in October 1881 at Skookum Bay in Mason County. A Squaxin shaman, Squs-sacht-un, who was named John Slocum by the white man, knelt in the woods to think of the error of his ways and the evil days that had overtaken him and his friends. Squs-sacht-un had lived a life of the "white man's vices:" horse racing, whiskey drinking, and idleness.

Squs-sacht-un became very ill and hovered near death for about two weeks while five Indian doctors tried to heal him. He died at four in the morning. His brother went to Olympia for a coffin and a grave was dug. Late the next afternoon, Squs-sacht-un recovered with a story to tell. Squs-sacht-un described an out-of-body experience where he looked down at his own dead body and saw he had no soul. He saw "a great light from that good land" where angels told him that he could not enter heaven because he was so wicked. He had a choice of going to hell or returning to earth to warn people to change their ways.

Squs-sacht-un was told he was given four days to live. He prayed the whole time until another voice told him he could live four weeks if he would build a church. The church was built and Squs-sacht-un was told he could live four years if he lived right. He did, combining Catholic and Native American doctrine and ceremony into the Shaker Church. They were called Shakers because their bodies would shake during the services as part of a healing ceremony to rid a person of sickness, sin, or both. James Wickersham, a Tacoma attorney, said in 1892 that Shaker Church members "practiced the strictest morality, sobriety and honesty. Their 600 members do not drink, gamble or race horses."

The formation of the Shaker Church was occurring at the same time as the Ghost Dance of the Sioux, which resulted in their persecution and ultimately the US Army's massacre of nearly three hundred Lakota People on December 29, 1893 at Wounded Knee. The Shaker Church was strongly opposed by their Indian agent at the time, Edwin Eells, and his missionary brother, the Rev. Myron Eells. They banished Squs-sacht-un and his associates from their reservation, then imprisoned them in chains in a single-room jail at the Indian Agency in Puyallup.

As the National Park Service explains:

> The Dawes Act (sometimes called the Dawes Severalty Act or General Allotment Act), passed in 1887 under President Grover Cleveland, allowed the federal government to break up tribal lands. The federal government aimed to assimilate Native Americans into mainstream US society by encouraging them towards farming and agriculture, which meant dividing tribal lands into individual plots. Only the Native Americans who accepted the division of tribal lands were allowed to become US citizens. This ended in the government stripping over 90 million acres of tribal land from Native Americans, then selling that land to non-native US citizens.

In addition, land-holding, tax-paying Indians were no longer wards of the state or under the control of Indian agents. Squssucht-un was freed.

The Shaker religion spread to Native American communities across western Washington. In 1890, a Shaker church was built at Jamestown. In 1921, the largest group of Shakers to ever assemble was at a convention at Jamestown. No one thought there'd be so many mouths to feed. The Shakers prayed. As the tide went out, hundreds of humpies were stranded in the eelgrass on the tide flats. It's said in the old days, salmon were stranded on the tide flats every summer, but no one had seen this happening for twenty-five years before the Shaker Convention.

In 1967, an estimated 400,000 humpies ran up the Dungeness River. While this year's run of humpies isn't that big, the fact that there's one humpy left after a century of gross mismanagement of this fishery is a miracle—a miracle of the salmon.

September 1, 2021

38

THE BLUE-TARP CAMPER

The blue-tarp camper is named for a particular shade of inexpensive, blue plastic tarp that comes in various shapes and sizes. Blue-tarp campers celebrate our pioneer heritage, where less trouble means more enjoyment of outdoor adventures, no matter what the weather.

Last weekend, it rained in the rainforest. The blue-tarp campers thumbed their noses at the rain and the ostentatious displays of wanton materialism clogging our highways and campgrounds with monster McMotorhomes, fifth-wheels, trailers, campers, and that other aberration of the pioneer spirit, the rooftop tents.

The manufacturers of these monstrosities advertise them as "part treehouse and part glamping tent [and]…an intriguing alternative to traditional tents that you see pitched at most car campgrounds. You can find models to fit on top of your car or truck." This summer, the rooftop tents were all the rage among the motor campers, although I cannot imagine why. If climbing a skinny ladder up to the top of your vehicle to get into your rooftop tent sounds "intriguing," then climbing back out of the tent and down the ladder in the middle of the night to answer the call of nature sounds like a real outdoor adventure.

Manufacturers of the rooftop tents stress that it's a good idea to take down and secure the rooftop tent on top of your vehicle before driving away from your campsite. Duh. It was a sound piece of advice that was obviously ignored by a certain rooftop-tent camper seen motoring down US Highway 101 last weekend. The rooftop tent was still set up, spewing personal belongings on the roadway while providing amusement to the fellow motorists. To their credit, the rooftop tent was almost still standing at fifty-five miles per hour, which is good to know if you ever want to camp in a typhoon.

Blue-tarp campers don't have that problem. Our camps fold up into tight little bundles. We don't have to climb a ladder to hit the hay either. The blue-tarp camper wouldn't want to. We prefer the simple things in life. You can't sit by a campfire inside your rooftop tent or motorhome. You can watch a video of a campfire on your phone or big-screen TV, but it's just not the same. You're missing the essential elements of camping, such as being outside with the campfire smoke and sparks burning holes in your clothes.

A real blue-tarp camper doesn't need one of those sissy tents either. The typical camper's tent is a complicated device that was designed by someone with a sadistic sense of humor. Every summer, countless hours are spent in various attempts to set up the tents. Often, in a fit of frustration over broken poles, missing parts, and self-medication, the tent campers are forced to wrap the tent around them and sleep in a sort of three-season cocoon that's anything but comfortable.

A blue-tarp camper doesn't need any of that stuff. We hearken back to a simpler time, when you camped by your wits and a woodsman's skill. With nothing but a bungee cord and a blue tarp, you could rig a lean-to that reflected the light of the fire into the far corners of the shelter. There, in the stillness of the wilderness, you can listen to the night sounds of the summer rain, creatures stalking the camp, and voices of the river sliding slowly by. You can keep your rooftop tent and fancy tin boxes on wheels. We'll camp in the blue tarp any day.

September 2, 2022

39

WHO OWNS THE RIVER?

Tourists ask many questions about the Olympic Peninsula. How deep is the river? How tall is that tree? How much farther? One day a tourist asked a question that was really tough to answer.

"Who owns the Hoh River?" It began with the melting of the great continental ice sheet about fifteen thousand years ago. We can assume this land has been continually inhabited by Native peoples ever since. Why would they leave? The Olympic Peninsula was a paradise of seafood and big game that amounted to the ultimate surf and turf buffet with herbs, root crops, and berry side dishes all there for the taking.

People began fishing when the salmon arrived about nine thousand years ago. Our forests appeared about six thousand years ago in response to a shift to a colder, wetter climate. The people began making canoes about three thousand years ago. The first cedar plank houses were built over a thousand years ago.

By then, a Northwest Coast sea-going culture had developed that largely depended on salmon, seals, whales, and tidal resources for food and the cedar tree for a material culture that blossomed until the appearance of the Europeans.

The invasion of the west coast began in 1513 when Vasco Nunez de Balboa crossed the Isthmus of Panama, waded into the Pacific Ocean, and claimed possession of the sea and all the lands it touched for Spain. He was followed by English and American explorers and traders who came from the south while the Russians came from the north. All of them were looking for treasure, plunder, and territory to claim.

When it was discovered that there was no gold and it was apparent the sea otter would soon be eradicated, the Spanish interest in the northwest cooled. The Russians went broke. The Americans bluffed the British, leaving the United States owners of the Hoh River. At the time, there were seven villages of the Hoh people along the river from tidewater to the mountains. The entire watershed was used for hunting, fishing, foraging, spiritual rituals, and burials. The Russians shipwrecked on the Hoh River in 1809 mentioned thirteen canoes full of people passing downriver in one day indicating the Hoh was a very busy place.

In 1863, the Hoh tribe were forced to sign a treaty that moved them to Quinault, but they refused to abandon their homeland. President Grover Cleveland established the current 443-acre Hoh Reservation in 1893. By then, Europeans were claiming land along the Hoh River under the Homestead Act. The Hoh people could not homestead what had been their land because they were not US citizens at the time.

The Hoh River country was one of the last areas in America that were opened to homesteading where you could acquire title to 160 acres of land just by building a structure and cultivating a crop. That might sound easy enough, until you consider there were no roads, electricity, or diesel-powered heavy equipment to clear the massive stumps so you could build a structure and plant a crop. All supplies had to be back-packed across twenty some miles of muddy trail from Forks or pushed in a cedar dugout upriver with a long pole. Only the tough survived the forest fires, hurricanes, droughts, and floods that made life on the Hoh River a battle for survival.

This tradition of homesteading unclaimed land came to a crashing halt in 1897 when President Grover Cleveland established the two-million-acre Olympic Forest Reserve that encompassed almost two-thirds of the Olympic Peninsula.

By then, the elk on the Olympic Peninsula were well on their way to becoming an endangered species. In his 1885 expedition, Lt. Joseph P. O'Neil found large herds of elk up in the Hurricane Ridge country above Port Angeles that were so tame they wouldn't spook when members of his expedition shot at them. With the increasing human population, elk were market-hunted for their meat and killed for their ivory teeth, then the fashion on the watch fobs of members of the Benevolent and Protective Order of Elks. Elk Mountain, above Port Angeles, was named for a famous elk massacre where the elk were shot and left to rot. The elk left the area and never came back. In 1905, elk hunting was outlawed in Washington.

Meanwhile, under pressure from logging, mining, and railroad interests, President William McKinley and Congress reduced the size of the Forest Reserve by 750,000 acres in 1900. The Forest Lieu Act allowed railroads to exchange useless acres of sagebrush, deserts, and mountains given to them as a government subsidy for some of the most valuable stands of spruce, cedar, and Douglas fir in the Pacific Northwest.

By this time, the conservation movement was starting in the United States. When Theodore Roosevelt was elected President in 1901, he selected Gifford Pinchot, a Connecticut millionaire with a passion for saving forests, to lead the newly created Forest Service under the Department of Agriculture. Pinchot's goal was to regulate logging so that the harvest did not exceed the new growth of timber.

This balance between harvest and growth was threatened by the increasing wildfires that raged across the west from slash burning in logging and farming operations. The Forest Service began building a system of trails connecting to fire lookouts located throughout the Olympic Mountains used to spot the fires before they had a chance to spread.

Two days before leaving office in 1909, President Theodore Roosevelt was convinced by conservationists to sign an executive order creating the 620,000-acre Olympus National Monument to protect what was left of the elk. In 1915, President Woodrow Wilson cut the monument back to 328,000 acres in an effort to mine manganese for armaments in World War I. By the 1930s, the United States was plunged into the depths of the Great Depression.

In 1933, President Franklin D. Roosevelt created the Civilian Conservation Corps. The CCC was a voluntary public work relief program for young men that built trails and shelters throughout the Olympics. In 1938, President Roosevelt signed a bill creating Olympic National Park, which gave the National Park Service ownership of the upper Hoh River. In 1953, President Harry Truman added the coastal strip, which put the mouth of the Hoh River within the National Park.

The constantly changing nature of federal land management and a hurricane in 1921 that knocked down billions of board feet of timber all across the Olympic Peninsula made the large timber companies reluctant to build railroads into the Hoh River country. Meanwhile, the 355-mile-long Olympic Loop Highway, today's US Highway 101, was completed in 1931. This made it possible to truck logs from the Hoh River to previously unreachable markets. The Native Americans had been the first to log the Olympic Peninsula. They cut the western red cedar. Every part of the cedar tree, from its roots to the branches, was used by Native Americans before the days of European contact.

The aromatic wood was split into boards for cedar plank houses. Cedar logs were carved into canoes. Cedar bark was used for clothing. Cedar roots were weaved into baskets. Cedar limbs were dried and twisted into rope. Cedar buds, bark, and roots were used as medicines and in ceremonial rituals. When the first European homesteaders settled here, they used split cedar to build their houses and barns. If cedar was not available, the Sitka spruce could be used.

With the outbreak of World War I, spruce was in demand for use in airplane construction. The Hoh River pioneers split cants from spruce logs and floated them down to the mouth of the river, where the courageous Captain Hanks sailed them through the surf to a mill in Aberdeen. That was until he mentioned patching his ship *The Surf Duck* with linoleum and was never heard from again.

By the 1920s, a chemical process was discovered to make pulp out of hemlock, previously considered a weed tree. Meanwhile, a glue was invented that perfected the manufacture of plywood. This revolutionized the construction industry and created a lucrative market for Douglas fir "peelers," logs that could be peeled on a lathe into plywood. With the coming of World War II, logging increased to meet the higher demand for timber. Diesel replaced steam power. The chainsaw replaced the crosscut saw or "misery whip."

In the 1950s, the state Department of Natural Resources began selling forty-acre timber sales on the Peninsula. The Columbus Day storm of 1962 created a huge supply of downed timber that overwhelmed domestic sawmills. Coincidentally, the Japanese post-war economy had rebounded to the point where they were buying and exporting raw logs from the West Coast of the United States. The 1960s were a time of the biggest timber sales of up to twenty-five million board feet. Japanese log buyers were competing with one another for some of the most beautiful, tight-grained, knot-free wood in the world. By the 1970s, Forks became the self-proclaimed "Logging Capital of the World."

As the old-growth rainforest of hemlock, cedar, and spruce was cut, it was replaced by the Douglas fir. These fir trees grew fast and up to four feet taller, adding inches in diameter every year. Unfortunately, many of these fir trees could not adapt to their new home in the rainforest. They grew crooked trunks with three or four tops, spike knots, and other defects that made inferior lumber.

At the time, the red alder was considered a weed that competed with the Douglas fir. In an effort to eliminate the alder and anything else that would compete with the Douglas fir, the herbicide 2,4-d was sprayed from helicopters all across the Olympic Peninsula. These days, alder is used for furniture, making it more valuable than fir.

By the 1980s, the Japanese recession had cooled the log market. Environmental restrictions designed to protect the spotted owl, marbled murrelet, and bull trout stopped the harvest of old-growth timber. Logging communities all across the Pacific Northwest were devastated. Loggers had to either move away or reinvent themselves as prison guards or anything else that would pay the bills. Multinational timber companies began looking for ways to divest themselves from environmentally sensitive areas they couldn't log. This paved the way for yet another change in the ownership of the Hoh River.

Beginning in 2003, a consortium of non-governmental agencies under the leadership of the Hoh River Trust secured grants, loans, and private funding to purchase seven thousand acres of land along the Hoh River from Olympic National Park to the ocean. In 2017, the Hoh River Trust was facing financial difficulties. Suggestions to give the land back to the original owners, the Hoh Tribe, were ignored. Instead, it was decided to donate their land to the Nature Conservancy.

The Hoh River now belongs to state, federal, and county bureaucracies who, along with the myriad non-governmental organizations, operate under the general term of the salmon restoration industry. This is an industry whose gross incompetence, waste, and greed has managed the legendary fisheries of this last best river in America into threatened or endangered species status. The Hoh River used to feed people. It is now used to feed the salmon restoration industry, whose gratuitous research, make-work projects, and bloated budgets profit from the engineered extinction of salmon.

The Hoh River now belongs to the salmon restoration industry. This is an alternative universe filled with confusing acronyms and weaponized semantics (a resiliency resource is defined as a log in an engineered logjam) designed to defuse, deflect, and deny any criticism of the master plan. There is no oversight to the master plan. There is no way of measuring its success because there isn't any. Seeing the destruction of the fish runs on the Hoh River can make us unable to place the events in their historical perspective, but we can try.

People who were outraged by the slaughter of the estimated sixty million bison that once roamed our great plains simply could not understand how our nation's industrial revolution required bison bone for fertilizer and bison hides for conveyor belts lubricated with whale oil. They could not possibly accept that then, as now, extinction is good for business.

The Hoh River has been transformed through the best available science into a dying thing where bureaucrats, biologists, consultants, and non-governmental organizations circle overhead like vultures over a carcass. All of this is in an effort to pad their resumes and inflate their budgets with a modern version of the medieval divine right of kings, where they can do no wrong. Salmon restoration can never be questioned and they can never be held accountable for their destructive practices that are destroying the resource they are paid to protect. They own the Hoh River.

September 9, 2020

40

IT IS NEVER TOO LATE TO PANIC

As a student of wilderness survival, it has always amazed me how often wilderness survival experts offer the same wilderness survival advice: "don't panic." For example, if you are lost in the forest with night coming on and you hear the footsteps of a large creature that seems to be following you, don't panic.

If you should suddenly come face to face with an enraged cougar, bear, or nest of bald-faced hornets, don't panic. If you fall into a river or get swept out to sea by a riptide, don't panic. In fact, given the temperature of our water, you probably won't have time to panic before you lapse into hypothermia.

Personally, when it comes to wilderness survival, I like to panic at the first available opportunity. For example, once upon a time on a wilderness survival exercise disguised as a bird-watching trip, we discovered we had only coffee beans instead of ground coffee for the morning brew. Panic was inevitable. Panic can be a great motivator. In a state of advanced panic, I was able to smash the beans with an axe, ensuring a satisfying morning ritual.

In that particular instance, the ability to harness panic in a constructive manner saved the expedition from the disastrous and even dangerous consequences of running out of coffee in the wilderness.

This begs the question: Might it be possible to harness the power of panic in our daily lives? The answer should be obvious to anyone who just looked out the window and saw fresh snow in the mountains. This, along with other key seasonal indicators of the severity of the coming winter, such as the thickness of corn husks, the size and abundance of spiders, or the winter coats on the coyotes, was pointing to a disturbing repetition of last year's "snowpocalypse." You remember last winter. It was like living inside your freezer with the light turned off. Just remember, when it comes to surviving the coming hard winter, it's a good idea to panic early and often.

It takes a village to get ready for winter. A hard winter can have a way of bringing folks together. In fact, there is a tradition in this country of neighbors helping neighbors as a way of expressing solidarity against the elements while we provide a shining beacon of humanity by enduring this adversity together. Neighbors who have not spoken in years are often glad to see other neighbors if they find them stuck in a ditch in a snowstorm and are able to pull them out.

Getting to know your neighbors is a good first step in winter survival. You may want to make a list of things your neighbors should have in case you need to borrow them in an emergency, like batteries, toiletries, mineral water, and coffee.

In addition to the snow, cold, and darkness, winter weather can leave us without electrical power for many minutes at a time. Power outages can represent a traumatic, irreversible negative impact in our daily lives. People can be forced to endure being trapped together in the same house without television, computers, or phones once the batteries go dead.

That is the perfect time to panic. Without the presence of these electronic devices in our daily lives, we could be forced to revert back to the practice of talking to one another in a manner not unlike primitive societies once did in the dawn of our history. You were warned; prepare. This winter will be wet, cold, and dark. It is never too late to panic.

October 2, 2019

41

THE NIGHT BEFORE DUCK SEASON

With apologies to Clement C. Moore
T'was the night before duck season and all through the shack
not a creature was stirring, not even a quack;
The shotguns were stacked by the chimney with care
in hopes that the mallards would soon be there.
The hunters were all passed out in their beds,
snoring like banshees trying to waken the dead.
Then out of the swamp, an engine roared.
I jumped to my feet and opened the door.
The rain and the wind came crashing in
and I in my PJs was soaked to the skin.
Then out of the storm, a duck cop appeared.
He said, "I hope all you boys are legal this year."
I said, "First time for everything and we all know
that the straight and narrow is the way to go."
This could be true or just might be proving
that duck hunters lie when their lips are moving.
Soon it was daylight and time to go
where the birds dropped in like a blizzard of snow.

On honkers, on pintails, on mallards, and more,
swept in by the sea to land on the shore,
while we wished you with all our might,
a good season to all and to all a good flight!

October 11, 2023

42

A GOOD DAY'S FISHING

Have you ever had one of those days where nothing seems to go right, when everything you try, try, and try again ends in a dismal failure of confusion, blame, and lame excuse? Welcome to my world. Some people think that being a fishing guide must beat working for a living, that all you have to do is catch a couple of fish or make up a story that you caught a couple of fish. When all else fails, you can blame the government, the weather, or the tourists. The game goes on. You have to show up to play.

Failure is an option that can rear its ugly head at any time. A bad slump can be made even worse by the success and good fortune of others. Out on the river, nothing could be worse than sitting there watching fish being caught while you couldn't catch one if it was flopping around in the bottom of the boat.

Just when you think it couldn't get any worse, the ignorant tourist in the front of the boat yells, "Fish on!"

He jumps up as if electroshocked, almost tipping the boat over while reeling as fast as he possibly can. This twists the line into an impossible tangle that must be cut out and replaced with new line while everyone else is catching fish. Still, I was grateful we had finally hooked something, until it became obvious that his trophy catch of a lifetime was what we call a timber trout or a limb cod, otherwise known as a piece of wood stuck to the bottom of the river.

We break off the five-dollar lure, which causes five bucks worth of line to erupt in a tangle that must be cut out and replaced while the other valued client chimes, "Fish on!" This time, it's a tangle of someone else's line with a couple of pounds of algae, which can put up quite a battle in fast water. It is soon painfully obvious even to a tourist that this is not a fish.

So, I try to show them how it's done with a mighty kamikaze-hurricane cast, which somehow goes very wrong and sinks the single barbless hook in my back between the shoulder blades.

As much as I complain about the stupid, single barbless hook regulations, barbless hooks are a lot easier to pull out of your hide than the hooks with the barbs on them. Still, it's almost a toss-up as what is more embarrassing: walking around with a fishing lure stuck in your back where you cannot reach or asking a perfect stranger to pull it out with some rusty pliers.

Suddenly, miraculously, inexplicably, the fish were there. We started catching big, bright, silver salmon one after the other. We had a double-header, two on at once, when my phone rang.

It was a call I had been waiting for. Momma went home, but not to her house. We had to sell that to pay for her care in the home. She went to her real home. She sent me some fish as a way of saying everything is okay. I can't explain how the death of a friend or a loved one makes the fish bite, but it's happened way too many times to be a coincidence. My friends Harry, Dusty, Bruce, and D.J. have all sent me fish after they passed. If I said it once, I've said it a hundred thousand times, which would still not be enough: "Thanks, Ma. I really needed that."

October 18, 2017

43

A LEGEND OF THE LOST

This has been a banner year for lost and injured hikers. As of Labor Day, seventy-one people were rescued or recovered from Olympic National Park. That's a big job. Lost people could save a truck load of trouble if they'd just tell someone where they are going and when they're coming back. Carry the ten essentials of wilderness survival, which includes fire-starter and something to drink, eat, wear, navigate with, communicate with, and survive with in one of the toughest environments on earth, the Olympic Peninsula rainforest.

We are coming up to one of the best times to get lost: elk hunting season. Hunters are focused on the elk to the point where they ignore everything else until it starts getting dark, which can be at three in the afternoon on a stormy day.

This is the story of three elk hunters who took off at daylight on opening day of elk season, November 4, 1974 up the Sams River, a tributary of the Queets. Two of the hunters, a father and son, got lost and stayed that way until rescued on November 7. This pair of elk hunters did not have the recommended ten essentials for wilderness survival. All they had was a little cardboard box of raisins like you'd give out at Halloween, which they rationed at four per day.

The first day, they became lost in a canyon with night coming on. Their failed efforts to build a fire resulted in what they described as one long night. On the second day, they decided that since all rivers flowed west into the Pacific Ocean, they would follow a stream. That was until they found themselves at the bottom of an impassable gorge, where darkness caught them once again.

Luckily, they found a snag that would burn and were able to dry out their clothes on one side while the rain soaked the other. This was another long night. On the third day, they made their way out of the gorge and into a swamp. By this time, it was getting dark again. They found some blown-down timber that had a dry spot underneath where they built a fire and warmed up for the first time since they were lost.

That's when the mental and physical effects of the ordeal caught up with the father. He began shaking. He couldn't sleep. He said his heart felt strange. He knew time was running out for them. He described his state of exhaustion: he could only go ten steps until he had to lean against a tree and try not to go to sleep.

They heard voices in the trees and thought the babbling creeks were talking to them. Then, they heard a shot on a ridge above them. Howard Rotter and Cliff Hay, Clearwater loggers who had hunted and logged the country, had been alerted by a park ranger who asked for help searching for the lost hunters and got it. Howard and Cliff strapped on their pistols and took off through the woods, firing signal shots until they heard an answer.

Howard yelled at the pair to stay put. The father tried to walk toward Howard but he was in such a state of confusion, he walked off in the opposite direction. Luckily, Dad could not outrun the loggers. They gave the lost elk hunters some candy bars and hiked them up the ridge to a road where the rest of the search and rescue crew gave them dry clothes, hot coffee, and a helicopter ride to a hospital in Tacoma. They did not get an elk.

October 30, 2019

44

GETTING ALONG IN THE COUNTRY

An awful lot of city folks are moving to the country these days and they want to know how to get along with the country folk. This can be a problem. City folks want to make the country like the city they escaped. Country folks want the city folks to just leave things well enough alone. Each views the other across a deep divide of mistrust, envy, and fear, often for no good reason.

It's really pretty easy to get along in the country by just observing three simple rules: shut up, drive slowly, and mind your own business. The simple fact is that the city folks and the country folks are all the same critter, just different.

Just because the country folks have moss growing on their welcome mats doesn't mean they don't want visitors. No. It just means the welcome can be mighty wet. Country folks generally have a pot of hot coffee on for visitors and a good hot meal to go with it.

Sometimes, the food can be a little strange. We might have clams for breakfast and hotcakes for dinner. Deal with it. A good rule of thumb for city folks to observe might be for city folks to observe caution when country folk urge the visitors to try some tasty wild mushrooms they just picked.

Still, mushroom picking is a good way to supplement the grocery list with wild food that is free for the gathering. That was my excuse anyway before I was sucked into a neighborhood discord of drama and intrigue for which I was in no way responsible.

I was just minding my own business, driving slowly, and not talking to anyone. As I neared a forest that held the secret mushroom patch, I came around a bend in the road to observe a stand-off between a native of the country and a newcomer.

There, sitting in the middle of the road with its back to me sat a huge bear, staring at a llama not fifty feet away. I stopped. Seeing llamas in the wild was not unusual in the lower Hoh River country. It was wrong of me to tell the tourists the llamas were actually genetically modified elk. I know that now. How these exotic animals have survived in a rainforest full of bears and cougars for years on their own is a testament to just how tough these animals are. Llamas can weigh over four hundred pounds and the one standing in the road staring down the bear was that big or bigger. The bear was just as big as the llama.

There's no telling how long the stand-off might have lasted if I had not happened along. After a few seconds, the bear looked around, saw me and melted into the thick brush on the side of the road. The llama took off running down the road like there was a herd of bears after it.

I waited a bit so as to let the llama calm down, but it didn't. Down the road a bit farther, I encountered a family of friendly mushroom pickers that the llama had barely missed as it galloped frantically by. They wondered what I did to the llama. Another mile down the road, I met a fishing guide who had narrowly avoided a head-on collision with the llama. He asked what I did to the llama. This is how rumors get started. That's life in the country. Shut up, drive slowly, and mind your own business and you can still get in trouble.

November 11, 2019

45

LOGGERS I HAVE KNOWN

Loggers have gotten a bad reputation lately. They are blamed for everything from noise pollution to cutting down trees. Fair enough. Loggers do cut down trees. That might be a good thing. If you're reading this on paper, made from wood, inside a house built of wood, that's warm and toasty on a frozen morning because you have a wood stove, you should thank a logger and count your blessings. Maybe you're lucky enough to have indoor plumbing. What toilet is complete without toilet paper? Would aluminum foil be a sustainable substitute in this age of environmental awareness? Loggers do make noise, but one person's noise pollution is another person's job.

It seems as if people these days would rather have trees rot in the woods and make soil than give someone a job cutting lumber out of them. They believe it's the topsoil that grows trees. If that was true, then the world record-sized cedar, fir, hemlock, and spruce of the Olympic Peninsula rainforest would be growing someplace with topsoil, like Iowa. They don't. Our trees grow out of steep mountains of solid rock. That's where Clyde found us logging on the dawn of a frosty morning. We were trying to untangle a chunk of rusty wire rope with marlin spikes and hammers. All of this was part of an effort to salvage some old-growth windfalls, cut them into cants, and recycle them into someone's house.

"This reminds me of the last depression," Clyde observed. He should know. Clyde was born in a logging camp, grew up in the Great

Depression, then shipped overseas in the war (the big one: World War II). Then, he came home to make the post-war boom that made our country so cool. Clyde had logged more timber than we would ever see in our lifetimes. By then, Clyde was retired so he had plenty of time to "shoot the breeze" and we almost had enough sense to listen.

Our logging show was in a pleasant setting, with mossy rocks for benches around a stump fire where a Dutch oven full of elk stew bubbled to one side. There was plenty of hot coffee.

Clyde watched the proceedings for a while and said, "I've got just the thing you need in my truck."

That much was true. Inside the back of Clyde's truck was enough tools and survival equipment to build a cabin. He rummaged around for a while and came up with a magic tool: the black powder wedge. This was an antique explosive device about the size of a quart bottle that you filled with gunpowder, pounded into a log, and ignited. The explosion would then split the log lengthwise, saving us the trouble of cutting it into cants, in theory anyway. The trouble was it had been so long since Clyde had used the exploding wedge, he had forgotten just how much powder you should use.

"If it's worth doing, it's worth overdoing," Clyde said as he filled the wedge to the brim full of powder. Then, he pounded it into the end of a log while I hid behind a large stump. After several attempts to light the fuse, there was a loud *boom*. When the smoke cleared, I poked my head around the stump. The log was shattered into kindling sticks. Clyde was still standing there, wondering where I went off to. That was a good day's logging.

November 10, 2011

46

THE LIFE OF A GUIDE

There is peace at the end of the day in sitting before a crackling fire along a fast river beneath a big tree as the sunset paints the colors of the fall leaves to garish shades of red and giving thanks that you survived another day in the life of a fishing guide. City folks laugh and say being a fishing guide isn't work because you're just fishing and that's what you like to do anyway, but fishing and guiding are two different things. When most people go fishing, they usually don't expect to catch anything. People who travel to the Olympic Peninsula from all over the world to go on guided fishing trips do expect to catch something. They bring gigantic coolers and great expectations of catching a salmon.

This may be a lifelong dream they have only one day to fulfill. They expect a guide to make a sincere effort to catch a giant fish. If you can fake that, you may have a future as a fishing guide. Size does matter. People want to catch a fish that's bigger than the one their buddies caught. Exact figures can vary widely. Some fish continue to grow long after they are freezer burnt, but the sad fact is you have to catch a fish before you can brag about it. That's where I come in. I help people with fishing problems.

Disturbed people are constantly calling me for the fishing report. A while back, I got a call from a guy from back east. For me, back east always meant Montana, but this guy was farther back east than that: Chicago. He said he was an investigating journalist, film critic, and

111

all-around smart guy. While investigating the *Twilight* phenomena, he had stumbled upon my wilderness gossip column and decided I needed investigating. I was told that dealing with journalists was a lot like handling rattlesnakes: don't trust them or they will bite you. Then there is Mark Twain's warning to not pick a fight with someone who uses "ink by the barrel." So, I did.

I took a journalist fishing. He said he wanted to ask me some questions about guiding. Questions are the curse of the fishing guide because we constantly have to answer all kinds of them. Do I really have a guide school? Do the fishing trips include past-life regression therapy? Was I really an unlicensed relationship counselor? How can I find my Indian name? Where is my car? Where are my keys? Small wonder the guides have developed a series of hazing rituals for the clients that separate the true fishermen from the wannabes and keep them from asking annoying questions.

These hazing rituals usually involve a form of sleep deprivation where the valued client is roused from a sound sleep in the middle of the night and raced around in circles on muddy roads in the dark. This generally leaves the person disoriented to the point where they forget all about catching a fish. They just want a cup of coffee and a warm place to go to the bathroom. Instead, they are hustled into a boat and hurried downriver in the dark while the guide insists they levitate to avoid hitting rocks. It's no small wonder the journalist called me "a malignant sociopath spewing misanthropic venom in a crude attempt at humor." Someone finally understands. The journalist caught a salmon anyway, which was revenge enough for one day. It was good to be alive.

November 17, 2011

47

HUNTING WITH BO

Way back when, the Olympic elk were market hunted for their meat, antlers, hides, and ivory teeth or just shot and left by thrill-seeking lowlifes who liked to watch them fall. In 1905, the Washington state legislature stopped all elk hunting. In 1909, President Teddy Roosevelt preserved what is now Olympic National Park to save the elk. By 1937, the elk had expanded beyond the carrying capacity of many parts of their range. Elk were starving in the Hoh Valley. Washington opened an eight-day season in October and November in Clallam and Jefferson counties for any and all elk.

William D. Welch of the *Port Angeles Evening News,* the precursor of today's *Peninsula Daily News,* journeyed to the upper Hoh River that October to cover what he called the "Elk War." Welch described the "red helmeted army of 5,280 hunters waging war against the Roosevelt elk in the West End of the Olympic Peninsula."

As with any war, there were casualties. It was a common practice for hunters to surround the unsuspecting elk herd and open fire. This meant the hunters were often firing at each other while blazing away at the elk. One man died in a fusillade of bullets. A packhorse was shot while carrying an elk. In his book *The Last Wilderness,* Murray Morgan told of a dairy cow that was shot so many times, the farmer melted it down to salvage the lead after elk season was over. An estimated seven hundred elk were killed. The figure might have been much higher except for a sudden storm that dumped so much rain, hunting was out of the question.

Welch describes the sorry spectacle when thousands of soaking wet elk hunters descended upon nearby Forks, which had run out of whiskey before the elk season had even started. All Forks had left was some gin, which was never very popular on the frontier. Things have changed in the eighty-five years since that first elk season. These days there is plenty of whiskey in Forks, but good luck finding ammunition!

Meanwhile, there are so many bears, cougars, and human hunters in the woods that many elk have moved into the town of Forks for their health. Elk hunting has always been tough, even when there were a lot more elk. These days, getting an elk is like winning the lottery. You need an edge. Instead of seven hundred elk killed in the Hoh Valley, I'd estimate less than twenty were harvested in the entire watershed. This is my story.

I got my first elk back in the '70s, hunting with my cousin Bo. We were hunting in one of the stupidest places you could ever want to pack an elk out of: the Dry Creek Basin west of Lake Cushman. Not many of you reading this have ever quartered an elk in a blizzard, but if you did, Bo was the right man for the job. It took three days to pack the elk out. It should have taught us a lesson. Instead, we went on many more hunting trips. Bo was one of the toughest humans I ever met, wearing cowboy boots to pack into Goat Lake.

Then, I got the call. Bo had died of some obscure disease right during elk season. Talk about your bad timing. The next day, through a bizarre series of coincidences, we ran into a herd of elk. I told my hunting partner that Bo had sent them. We had an edge. We got a year's worth of meat. If I said it once, I said it a million times: Thanks Bo. I needed that.

November 10, 2023

48

A DIRTY THIRTIES THANKSGIVING

This is a story told to me by an old-timer who grew up on a homestead in the Olympic Mountains. He said this is how his family celebrated a Thanksgiving in the olden days.

It was back in the Depression, the Dirty Thirties. Pa had somehow got some turkey chicks that spring. The plan was to have them for Thanksgiving, Christmas, and all of our holiday dinners. It's a good thing we didn't know how hard raising turkeys was.

I thought a turkey for Thanksgiving would beat what we had the year before: a grouse split between the four of us. Last Christmas, we had a spawned-out salmon for Christmas dinner. It was rank no matter how much salt and pepper you put on it.

When Pa showed up from town with eight turkey chicks that spring, they were helpless little fuzz balls that had somehow survived the long trip home in a gunny sack on horseback. We put the chicks in a box full of dried moss behind the cook stove, which smelled terrific after a few days. Then, we gave them all names. There were eight turkeys so we named them after Santa's eight reindeer. The only problem was the turkeys all looked the same. We couldn't tell one from the other.

We fed the chicks cornmeal mush but one of them, we figured it was Dasher, looked a little peaked. Dasher didn't make it through the first week. Then we were down to seven turkeys.

Once the turkeys were big enough, we put them in the chicken house. They got along with the chickens at first, but after a little while, the turkeys got too big to stay inside all day. We had to turn them loose. That's when the trouble started.

They spent the day out in the woods catching bugs and taking dust baths. Pa figured it would save on feed letting the turkeys find their own grub, until a big bald eagle swooped in and got Prancer. Then, we were down to six turkeys.

The real trouble started once the turkeys got so big, we couldn't get them back in the chicken house at night. Right before sundown, they would fly up into the limbs of a big fir tree to roost. There must have been a raccoon living up in that tree, or maybe an owl got them. Next thing you know, there was a pile of feathers on the ground and Comet and Cupid were missing.

That summer, what was left of the turkeys started serenading us with their gobble-gobble call, which acted like a dinner bell to every varmint in the country. Donner disappeared.

The coyotes got Blitzen and Dancer. Then, we only had only one turkey left. She was a big hen we had named Vixen. We changed her name to Lucky and locked her in the chicken house for safekeeping. Lucky got some extra grain to fatten up before the big Thanksgiving dinner.

As Thanksgiving approached, we were excited about our big dinner. Ma wanted a sage dressing. Pa wanted oyster dressing made with some canned smoked oysters he'd been saving for a special occasion. There was quite a disagreement, but us kids didn't care what kind of dressing we had as long as we had a turkey dinner.

The morning before the big day, Pa came into the house with bad news. Something broke into the hen house and Lucky was gone. Pa left the house with a shotgun and came back long after dark with a big blue grouse for Thanksgiving dinner. We all gave thanks at our Thanksgiving dinner. Pa said it's better to give thanks for what you have than feel sorry for what you don't.

November 27, 2019

49

RAIN

People come from all over the world to the west end, or what we call the wet end, of the North Olympic Peninsula to visit the rainforest so they can complain about the weather. It's my job as a fishing guide on the cutting edge of the tourism industry to reassure our atmospherically challenged guests so they do not feel victimized by current climactic conditions. It's been said the Eskimos have fifty different words for snow. Meteorologists and fishing guides have at least that many words for rain. These include driving rain, freezing rain, rain mixed with snow, and many names that cannot be printed in a family newspaper. It has been raining so much lately the old-timers have been wondering if it is time to start building a really big boat in the back yard. Don't bother.

In the beginning, God sent a Pineapple Express that lasted forty days and forty nights and drowned anything outside of Noah's Ark. After the water receded from the record flood levels, God set a rainbow in the sky as a promise he wouldn't drown the earth no matter how much measurable precipitation was recorded. Since then, periodic rainfall events have been a blessing. Without a seasonal moisture trend, there would be no rainforest. We need periodic gully washers to hatch the slugs, sprout the mushrooms, and make the skunk cabbage bloom.

This is the story of the seasonally adjusted jet stream pushing warm moisture-laden air up and over the icy mass of the Olympic

117

Mountains with a resulting release of atmospheric moisture. Significant moisture accumulations flow down the slope to form rivers. Without rivers, there would be no fish and if I couldn't fish, I'd have very little to write about.

That is why it is extremely fortunate that I am able to fish when it is too wet to work. With the recent spell of wet weather, it's almost impossible to get any chores done. There's just no way you can plow the garden, mow the lawn, or chop the firewood when an intense low-pressure system carrying lots of moisture from the Gulf of Alaska collides with a frigid high-pressure body of Frazier River outflow winds and stalls on top of you. The fact is, you can still go fishing in isolated showers that may be heavy at times and develop into freezing rain with a likely chance of afternoon thundershowers in some regions of the forecast area. That's when my tourist friends are likely to ask the craziest questions, like, "Does it ever stop raining here?"

Last time I heard that, we were floating downriver through the vapors of a lovely rainforest morning. It was still dark so it was easy for a/the tourist to think it was raining. I had to explain to my soggy friend that there could be a chance of heavy, localized showers later in the day. But rain? No, what we were experiencing was a blinding drizzle. There's a fine line between drizzle and a light shower. Often by using appropriate atmospheric terminology, visitors to the Olympic Peninsula will come to understand that being wet is cool. In fact, if it doesn't rain in the rainforest, you've been cheated out of a real nature experience.

December 1, 2019

50

THE OZETTE POTATO

Potatoes must be my favorite thing to dig, next to clams, but clam season is closed so I'm digging potatoes. I know what you're thinking. People are supposed to dig potatoes in the fall when the vines ripen and die down. But what if you're too busy fishing? Then you dig potatoes in the winter. That's the best time to dig them in this country. Spuds get soft if they are stored improperly, but if you keep them in the ground they stay hard as rocks. You may lose a few to the mice, but that is a small price to pay. Some may freeze and rot, but for the most part, a light frost gives the tubers a sweet taste that is impossible to buy in a plastic bag.

There are many types of taters—red, white, blue, and yellow—but my favorite is the Ozette potato, *Solanum tuberosum*. It isn't the biggest tater in the patch, but it stays hard and fresh until spring, with a sweet, creamy flavor the foodies tell us tastes vaguely like a chestnut. We'll take their word for it. All I know is the Ozette potato is a living piece of Olympic Peninsula history that goes back to May 29, 1791.

That's when Salvador Fidalgo, captain of the *Princessa*, anchored in Neah Bay with some seventy seamen and thirteen soldiers. Fidalgo had been sent with instructions to monitor shipping in the Strait of Juan de Fuca and build shelters, an infirmary, storehouses, and an oven to bake bread for the crews of visiting Spanish ships that were anticipated to reinforce their claims to the land.

Nunez Gaona is considered the first settlement by Europeans in the American Pacific Northwest. There were seven Peruvian Indians aboard the *Princessa,* so we might assume they brought the potatoes for vegetable gardens. A member of the nightshade family, it is estimated that the potato has been cultivated in South America for eight thousand to ten thousand years.

The Spanish conquistadors invaded South America looking for gold, but they also found the potato. The value of the humble potato has probably exceeded the wealth of precious metals since then. Those were the good old days when all you had to do to own land was plant a cross and claim you owned it. The problem was that Spain, England, Russia, and the United States all claimed the Olympic Peninsula that we now call home. The Nootka Convention of 1790 allowed joint occupation by British and Spanish invaders in the vast area we call the Pacific Northwest. This was a diplomatic effort to avoid yet another of the wars in Europe that had devastated the continent.

Nunez Gaona was not a happy place. The anchorage was treacherous. There was no gold. A Spanish first mate was killed. In a case of random retaliation, Capt. Fidalgo blew a canoe containing a Makah family out of the water. Two children survived. Fidalgo realized his position was untenable. Nunez Gaona only lasted three months. The potato stayed.

The Makah grew the potato instead of gathering camas. They traded garments of woven cedar bark, dog hair, and bird feathers for Hudson Bay blankets. They exchanged spears and the bow and arrow for firearms. It was part of the Manifest Destiny cultural grab bag that included alcohol, smallpox, and the Bureau of Indian Affairs. For more than two hundred years, the Makah kept the Ozette potato for us to remember and enjoy today. The Makah traditionally dipped their potatoes in whale or seal oil, but since the passage of the Marine Mammal Protection Act, we'll have to settle for the garlic butter.

December 10, 2019

51

YES, VIRGINIA, WE WILL SAVE THE ORCA

(With apologies to Francis Pharcellus Church, editor of *The New York Sun*, December 1897.)

Dear Editor,

I am eight years old. Some of my friends say we will not be able to save the orca or the salmon that feed them. My papa says, "if you see it in the Wilderness Gossip Column, it must be so." Please tell the truth. Will we save the orca?

Virginia,
Oil City

Virginia,

Your little friends are wrong. They have been affected by the fake news of our times. They do not believe they will be able to catch salmon in the future because they cannot catch them now. They think this is incomprehensible because just a few years ago, humans and the orca could catch all the fish they wanted. Just remember, the Earth has been here for billions of years while humans have been here since the day before yesterday, geologically speaking. Humans are greedy insects powerless to control their unbridled lust to subdue and plunder the boundless world about them. They are as unable to grasp the truth and knowledge of the tragedy of their deeds as they are to reverse them for the common good of the planet.

Yes, Virginia, we will save the orca and the salmon they depend on as certainly as we will save the other endangered species we are creating daily with our busy modern lives. Alas, how dreary would be the world if there were no orca. It would be as dreary as if there were no Virginia. Don't believe we will restore the orca and the salmon? You might as well not believe in fairies, leprechauns, and the tax break for the middle class. Have your father hire people to fish the rivers. If they do not catch a salmon, does that mean there aren't any? Half the people who go fishing don't catch one. What does that prove? Just because you cannot catch a salmon does not mean they are not there.

Believe. The orca and the salmon will be restored just as surely as there are leprechauns hiding buckets of gold at the end of the rainbow. You can tear apart one of the engineered logjams we have spent a fortune making and wonder where the salmon are. But our childlike faith tells us that just because building logjams hasn't brought the salmon back so far doesn't mean it cannot happen. No one can understand how we can spend so much money and have so few salmon to show for it. It is one of the unseen wonders of the modern world.

We must push aside that veil and view the logjams for their unnatural beauty and the prevailing wage jobs they provide. If we just keep spending billions more building more logjams, the salmon will come back, someday, somewhere. Our government agencies and career politicians do not lie for money. Only by continuing to build more log jams, buy more property (from willing sellers), plant more native vegetation, and spray more herbicides can we see that even if this does not bring the salmon back, we'll keep on trying as long as the money lasts.

Even if we should have no salmon except on paper, then we should still have that noble creature the sea lion. Let the orca eat sea lions. No salmon, no orca? That's ridiculous. Thank God they will live forever. A thousand years from now, nay ten times ten thousand years from now, the orca and the salmon will swim together. The only question is: Will humans still be around?

December 25, 2018

52

FISH ARE GETTING SMARTER

The American author John Steinbeck said, "It has always been my private conviction that any man who puts his intelligence up against a fish had it coming." He should know. Steinbeck spent much of the Great Depression fishing and crabbing out of a small boat in order to get enough food for him and his wife to survive. There is nothing on earth like subsistence fishing to humble a person into realizing that, on any given day, the fish can be smarter than he or she is. Over the years, Steinbeck's observations evolved into some of the earliest notions of the environmental movement.

A lot of this realization occurred to Steinbeck when he was hiding out from what he described as "land owners, bankers and death threats" after writing his 1939 masterpiece *The Grapes of Wrath*. The book was banned for being obscene and misrepresentative and remains so in parts of this experiment in democracy we call America.

In 1940, Steinbeck decided to get out of town. He and his marine biologist buddy Ed Ricketts went to the Gulf of California in the seiner *Western Flyer* to collect biological specimens. Once there, Steinbeck watched trawlers dragging their nets across the sea bed (a destructive practice that continues to this day), which illustrated the interconnection of humans and the environment. The resulting book, *Sea of Cortez*, was not a bestseller. However, the *Western Flyer* still survives to this day in Port Townsend, where it has been in the process of being restored since 2015. But I digress.

This is about the intelligence of fish, which can be greater than a human's intellect on any given day. It only makes sense. Research has indicated the intelligence of fish matches or exceeds that of the higher vertebrates, including nonhuman primates and some fishing guides on any given day. This should come as no surprise. Fish appeared in the fossil record about 530 million years ago. The first early modern humans may have appeared a scant 300,000 years ago. In the evolutionary scheme of things, if the history of the fish was the length of the Hood Canal Bridge, the history of humans would be a speed bump at the end of the bridge.

Many believe that the intelligence of fish is evolving at the precise rate that humans are getting dumber. Olympic Peninsula salmon and steelhead routinely navigate many thousands of miles across the ocean to the Aleutian Islands, returning years later to the precise stream where they were born. I get lost in parking lots.

Once in their home rivers, fish use rocks to break the speed of the current to navigate upstream without fighting the main force of the river. I hit the rocks going downstream. Fish use rocks to break fishing lines and dislodge any lures they're hooked on. I had to go to the emergency room at the Forks Community Hospital to have a hook removed. Fish use gravel in the bottom of the rivers to build nests across the streambeds that once stretched from the Rocky Mountains to the Pacific Ocean. The last time I made a nest in the gravel, I was drunk.

Recently, we witnessed a quantum leap in fish intelligence when a large steelhead was hooked. The line went slack. The fish was lost. The unfortunate angler reeled in his line to find a pigtail looking piece at the end. To the untrained eye, it looked like the knot on the lure came undone. That's impossible since I tied that knot myself. That would never happen. There was only one explanation: fish are getting smarter. Now they can untie knots, underwater, with no hands! Fishing is bound to get a whole lot tougher.

December 31, 2023

Printed in the United States
by Baker & Taylor Publisher Services

Printed in the United States
by Baker & Taylor Publisher Services